COLLINS

PICTURE
ATLAS
of the
WORLD

HarperCollins Children's Books
A division of HarperCollins Publishers Ltd,
77—85 Fulham Palace Road, Hammersmith, London W6 8JB

First published in the United Kingdom in 1994

Copyright © 1994 Orpheus Books Ltd

Text consultant: G R Peter Lawrence
Illustrations by Gary Hincks and Steve Noon *(Garden Studio)*

Created and produced by Nicholas Harris and Joanna Turner, Orpheus Books Ltd

ISBN 0 00 196570-0 (hardback)
ISBN 0 00 196571-9 (paperback)

A CIP record is available from the British Library

Printed and bound in Belgium

COLLINS

PICTURE
ATLAS
of the
WORLD

Written and designed by
Nicholas Harris

Illustrated by
Gary Hincks
&
Steve Noon

HarperCollins*Children'sBooks*

CONTENTS

KEY TO ILLUSTRATIONS

Left-hand column, top Cheese-porters, Alkmaar market, The Netherlands *centre* Arches National Park, Utah, USA *bottom* Sydney Harbour Bridge and Opera House, Australia *Right-hand page, top* Elephant mask, Cameroon *centre* Royal palace, Bangkok, Thailand *bottom* Machu Picchu, Peru *Along bottom of page* The Kremlin, Moscow, Russia

ABBREVIATIONS AND
SYMBOLS USED IN THIS ATLAS

Br.	(Great) Britain
Fr.	France
I.	Island
Is.	Islands
km	kilometres
L.	Lake
m	metres
Mt.	Mount
Mts.	Mountains
Neths.	Netherlands
Pop.	Population
Port.	Portugal
Rep.	Republic
sq km	square kilometres
U.A.E.	United Arab Emirates
U.S.	United States
★	National capital
④	Numbers in circles show where the subjects illustrated can be found on the maps

THE WORLD

Greenland

Ellesmere I.

Wrangel I.

Baffin Bay

Victoria I.

Baffin I.

Iceland

Mackenzie

Bering Sea

Hudson Bay

Aleutian Is.

Bri Isl

NORTH

St. Lawrence

Rocky Mountains

Missouri

Newfoundland

PACIFIC OCEAN

AMERICA

Azores

Mississippi

Bermuda

Canary Is.

Hawaiian Is.

Gulf of Mexico

ATLANTIC

OCEAN

Caribbean Sea

West Indies

Cape Verde Is.

Marshall Is.

Equator

Kiribati

Galápagos Is.

Amazon

Western Samoa

American Samoa

Andes

SOUTH

Ascens

Fiji

Pitcairn I.

AMERICA

Tonga

Cook Is.

French Polynesia

Easter I.

Paraná

Andes

New Zealand

Tristan Cunho

Falkland Is.

FACTS ABOUT THE WORLD

Circumference at the Equator 40,075 km
Land area 148,328,100 sq km
Ocean area 361,741,000 sq km
Population 5,477,000,000
Highest point Mt. Everest (Nepal and China) 8863 m
Greatest depth Marianas Trench 10,924 m
Lowest point on land Dead Sea (Israel and Jordan) 395 m below sea level
Longest river Nile (Africa) 6670 km
Largest lake Caspian Sea 371,000 sq km
Largest country Russia 17,075,400 sq km
Largest population China 1,141,530,000
Largest city Mexico City (Mexico) 15,000,000 people

South Georgia

ARCTIC OCEAN

Severnaya
Zemlya

Svalbard

Novaya
Zemlya

Norwegian
Sea

Ob

Yenisey

Lena

Sea of
Okhotsk

North
Sea

EUROPE

Volga

Irtysh

Amur

Kuril Is.

Gobi

Black Sea

Caspian
Sea

A S I A

Honshu

Mediterranean
Sea

▼ Dead
Sea

Himalayas

▲ Mt.
Everest

Yangtse

PACIFIC

OCEAN

a h a r a

Nile

Arabian
Sea

Bay of
Bengal

South
China
Sea

Northern
Mariana
Is.

Niger

AFRICA

Philippine
Is.

▼ Marianas
Trench

Gulf of
Guinea

Zaire

Maldive
Is.

Borneo

Palau

Marshall
Is.

New Guinea

Nauru

Sumatra

Seychelles

Cocos
I.

Java

Solomon
Is.

Madagascar

St. Helena

Mauritius

INDIAN

Réunion

OCEAN

Vanuatu

AUSTRALIA

New
Caledonia

Tasman
Sea

New
Zealand

Kerguelen
Is.

SOUTHERN OCEAN

ANTARCTICA

UNITED KINGDOM
 ICELAND
 NORWAY
 SWEDEN
 FINLAND
 DENMARK
 POLAND
 GERMANY
 AUSTRIA

 IRELAND
 NETHERLANDS
 BELGIUM
 LUXEMBOURG
 FRANCE
 SWITZERLAND
 MONACO
 ITALY
 VATICAN CITY
 SAN MARINO
 MALTA
 ANDORRA
 PORTUGAL
 SPAIN
 LIECHTENSTEIN
 HUNGARY
 BULGARIA
 ALBANIA
 GREECE
 SLOVENIA
 CROATIA
 MACEDONIA

EUROPE

EUROPE AND ASIA together form one vast land mass called Eurasia. Europe itself lies west of the Ural Mountains, to the north of the Caucasus and on the western bank of the Bosporus strait. A large part of Russia and a small area of Turkey both fall within Europe.

Europe is a land of peninsulas and islands surrounded by the waters of the North Atlantic Ocean and its seas. The ocean has a great effect on the climate of the north-western countries, giving them wet, but also milder, winters. Central and eastern Europe have greater extremes of temperature: hot in summer but bitterly cold in winter. The lands bordering the Mediterranean Sea enjoy hot, dry summers and mild winters.

Nearly every corner of the continent which is not too mountainous or infertile has been shaped by humans, either farmed for crops, turned over to pasture, or built over with towns and cities, roads, airports, quarries or factories. Europe is densely populated, particularly in the lowland regions of western Europe where industrial cities have grown up close to one another.

Eastern European countries are generally not as prosperous as those in the west. Along with the former Soviet Union, some have recently broken up into smaller nations.

ICELAND

Bearded seal

Fishing

FAEROE IS.
(Denmark)

Killer whale

Fishing

NORTH SEA

Whisky distillery

Oil

Skiing

Pigs

Sheep

Pigs

IRELAND

UNITED KINGDOM

DENMARK

Cattle

Fishing

Gas

Coal

NETHERLANDS

Cattle

Channel Tunnel

BELGIUM

Kiel C

Industry

LUXEMBOURG

GERMANY

Cattle

Sugar beet

Beer

Grapes

Wheat

Skiing

FRANCE

SWITZERLAND

Tobacco

Car factory

Wheat

PORTUGAL

Pigs

ANDORRA

Grape harvest

Grape

Fishing

Sheep

Grapes

ATLANTIC OCEAN

SPAIN

Tourism

Sheep

GIBRALTAR
(Br.)

Oranges

MEDITERRANEAN SEA

Lemons

Tourism

CZECH REPUBLIC

SLOVAKIA

FACTS ABOUT EUROPE

Area 9,700,000 sq km
Population 695,000,000
Highest point Elbrus (Russia) 5664 m
Lowest point Caspian Sea (Russia) 28 m below sea level
Longest river Volga (Russia) 3668 km
Largest lake Ladoga (Russia) 17,700 sq km
Largest country (excluding Russia) Ukraine 603,700 sq km
Largest population (excluding Russia) Germany 79,753,000
Largest city Moscow (Russia) 8,769,000 people

Mining

Lapp herdsman

Mining

White Sea

Elk

FINLAND

L. Ladoga

Timber

Timber

SWEDEN

Mechanical log cutter

Brown bear

Wolf

RUSSIA

Mining

Aircraft factory

ESTONIA

Potatoes

Cattle

Wheat

Oil

Volga

LATVIA

Cattle

BALTIC SEA

LITHUANIA

Flax

Maize

RUSSIA

BELARUS

Sugar beet

Potatoes

Pigs

Potatoes

POLAND

Chernobyl Nuclear power station

Wheat

Coal

Horse-drawn plough

UKRAINE

Coal

Herding cattle

Tobacco

Caspian Sea

CH REPUBLIC

Harvesting wheat

Mining

SLOVAKIA

Sheep

Elbrus ▲

AUSTRIA

Grapes

Pigs

MOLDOVA

HUNGARY

Gas

SLOVENIA

Wheat

CROATIA

ROMANIA

BOSNIA

Ferry

BLACK SEA

SERBIA AND MONTENEGRO

Grapes

Sheep

Grapes

BULGARIA

Grapes

T U R K E Y

ITALY

Olives

MACEDONIA

Tobacco

ALBANIA

Aegean Sea

GREECE

Olives

Tourism

CYPRUS

RUSSIA

ESTONIA

LATVIA

LITHUANIA

BELARUS

UKRAINE

MOLDOVA

ROMANIA

THE EUROPEAN UNION

Twelve countries form the European Union. They are: Belgium, Netherlands, Luxembourg, Germany, France, Italy, United Kingdom, Ireland, Denmark, Spain, Portugal and Greece. Once known as the European Community, these countries now trade goods freely with one another. Norway, Sweden, Finland and Austria join in 1995.

BOSNIA

CYPRUS

SERBIA & MONTENEGRO

NATIONS OF EUROPE

ALBANIA
Area 27,398 sq km **Population** 3,300,000
Capital Tiranë **Language** Albanian

ANDORRA
Area 468 sq km **Population** 55,000 **Capital**
Andorra **Languages** Catalan, French, Spanish

AUSTRIA
Area 83,859 sq km **Population** 7,712,000
Capital Vienna **Language** German

BELARUS
Area 207,600 sq km **Population** 10,260,000
Capital Minsk **Language** Belorussian

BELGIUM
Area 30,519 sq km **Population** 10,022,000
Capital Brussels **Languages** Dutch (Flemish),
French, German

BOSNIA
Area 51,129 sq km **Population** 4,365,000
Capital Sarajevo **Language** Serbo-Croat

BULGARIA
Area 110,994 sq km **Population** 8,989,000
Capital Sofia **Languages** Bulgarian, Turkish,
Macedonian

6 Irish boy

CROATIA
Area 56,538 sq km **Population** 4,700,000
Capital Zagreb **Language** Serbo-Croat

CYPRUS
Area 9251 sq km **Population** 527,000 **Capital**
Nicosia **Languages** Greek, Turkish, English

CZECH REPUBLIC
Area 78,864 sq km **Population** 10,302,000
Capital Prague **Language** Czech

DENMARK
Area 43,093 sq km **Population** 5,162,000
Capital Copenhagen **Language** Danish

ESTONIA
Area 45,125 sq km **Population** 1,575,000
Capital Tallinn **Languages** Estonian, Russian

FINLAND
Area 338,145 sq km **Population** 5,029,000
Capital Helsinki **Languages** Finnish, Swedish

FRANCE
Area 543,965 sq km **Population** 57,049,000
Capital Paris **Language** French

GERMANY
Area 356,854 sq km **Population** 79,753,000
Capitals Berlin, Bonn **Language** German

GREECE
Area 131,957 sq km **Pop.** 10,020,000
Capital Athens **Language** Greek

HUNGARY
Area 93,030 sq km **Population** 10,337,000
Capital Budapest **Language** Hungarian

ITALY
Area 301,277 sq km **Pop.** 57,746,000
Capital Rome **Language** Italian

LATVIA
Area 64,589 sq km **Population** 2,606,000
Capital Riga **Languages** Latvian, Russian

1 Sami (Lapp) boy from Norway

★ Capital city

Scale
0   600 km

REYKJAVIK ICELAND

NORWEGIAN SEA

ATLANTIC OCEAN

FAEROE IS.
(Denmark)

TRONDHEIM

BERGEN

NORTH SEA

OSLO

GÖTEBORG

STOCK

GLASGOW EDINBURGH
BELFAST NEWCASTLE

IRELAND UNITED
DUBLIN LEEDS
MANCHESTER KINGDOM
BIRMINGHAM

DENMARK

COPENHAGE

HAMBURG

CARDIFF LONDON AMSTERDAM
NETHERLANDS HANNOVER BERLIN
BELGIUM ESSEN Elbe
LILLE BRUSSELS BONN GERMANY
LUXEMBOURG FRANKFURT PRAGU
PARIS STRASBOURG STUTTGART CZECH REPU
NANTES Loire MUNICH VIENNA
FRANCE BERN ZÜRICH BRATI
Bay of LIECHTENSTEIN AUSTRIA
Biscay SWITZERLAND
BORDEAUX SLOVENIA
LYON MILAN LJUBLJANA ZA
PORTO BILBAO TURIN CROA
MARSEILLE MONACO BO
SAN MARINO SARAJEV
LISBON PORTUGAL Tagus MADRID ANDORRA Corsica ROME
SPAIN BARCELONA
VALENCIA Sardinia NAPLES
PALMA
SEVILLA Mallorca CAGLIARI
GIBRALTAR
(Br) MEDITERRANEAN SEA PALERMO
Sicily
MALTA

Gd

Szcz
P

Wro

5

English Channel

Rhine

Ebro

Adriatic

5 Gypsy girl from Italy

ICELAND
Area 103,000 sq km **Population** 260,000
Capital Reykjavik **Language** Icelandic

IRELAND
Area 70,283 sq km **Population** 3,523,000
Capital Dublin **Languages** English, Irish

LIECHTENSTEIN
Area 160 sq km **Population** 29,000
Capital Vaduz **Language** German

LITHUANIA
Area 65,200 sq km **Population** 3,761,000
Capital Vilnius **Languages** Lithuanian,
Russian, Polish, Belorussian

LUXEMBOURG
Area 2586 sq km **Population** 390,000
Capital Luxembourg **Languages** German,
Letzeburgesch, French

MACEDONIA
Area 25,713 sq km **Pop.** 2,179,000 **Capital**
Skopje **Languages** Macedonian, Albanian

MOLDOVA
Area 33,700 sq km **Population** 4,361,000
Capital Kishinev **Languages** Romanian
(Moldovan), Ukrainian, Russian

MONACO
Area 2 sq km **Population** 30,000
Language French

NORWAY
Area 323,877 sq km **Population** 4,250,000
Capital Oslo **Language** Norwegian

POLAND
Area 312,683 sq km **Population** 38,183,000
Capital Warsaw **Language** Polish

PORTUGAL
Area 92,389 sq km **Population** 10,525,000
Capital Lisbon **Language** Portuguese

ROMANIA
Area 237,500 sq km **Population** 22,761,000
Capital Bucharest **Languages** Romanian,
Hungarian, German

RUSSIA
Area 17,075,400 sq km **Population**
148,543,000 **Capital** Moscow
Languages Russian, 38 other languages

SAN MARINO
Area 60.5 sq km **Population** 24,000
Language Italian

SERBIA AND MONTENEGRO
Area 102,350 sq km **Population** 9,950,000
Capital Belgrade **Languages** Serbo-Croat,
Albanian, Hungarian

SLOVAKIA
Area 49,035 sq km **Population** 5,310,000
Capital Bratislava **Languages** Slovak,
Hungarian, Czech

SLOVENIA
Area 20,251 sq km **Population** 2,020,000
Capital Ljubljana **Language** Slovene

SPAIN
Area 504,782 sq km **Population** 39,322
Capital Madrid **Languages** Spanish, Catalan,
Basque, Galician

2 Lithuanian girl

3 Ukrainian girl

4 Slovak boy from the
Czech Republic

SWEDEN
Area 449,964 sq km **Population** 8,644,000
Capital Stockholm **Languages** Swedish, Finnish,
Lappish

SWITZERLAND
Area 41,293 sq km **Population** 6,751,000
Capital Bern **Languages** German, French,
Italian

UKRAINE
Area 603,700 sq km **Population** 51,944,000
Capital Kiev **Languages** Ukrainian, Russian

UNITED KINGDOM
Area 242,533 sq km **Population** 57,411,000
Capital London **Languages** English, Welsh

VATICAN CITY
Area 0.44 sq km **Pop.** 800 **Language** Italian

MALTA
Area 316 sq km **Population** 360,000
Capital Valletta **Languages** Maltese,
English, Italian

NETHERLANDS
Area 33,936 sq km **Population** 15,065,000
Capitals Amsterdam, The Hague
Language Dutch

NORTHERN EUROPE

NORWAY, SWEDEN AND DENMARK are often grouped under the name Scandinavia. Taken together with Finland and Iceland these are the Nordic countries of Europe. All except Denmark reach northward to Arctic latitudes. Here is the 'Land of the Midnight Sun', so-called because the sun never sets during the summer months. Very cold temperatures are recorded in the far north tundra regions *(see page 76)*, but the coast of Norway is warmed by currents from tropical waters, and is quite mild in winter.

High mountains run down the spine of the Scandinavian peninsula and broaden to fill nearly all of southern Norway. On the west coast, long, deep arms of the sea called fjords fill mountain valleys carved out by glaciers. All except Denmark reach forested slopes run down to the Gulf of Bothnia. In both Sweden and Finland tens of thousands of lakes have formed where glaciers have scooped out valleys or hollows in the land and the ice has later melted.

2 In the summer, herds of reindeer move north from the forests to graze in pastures.

3 Glass-blowing, a traditional industry of both Sweden and Finland

1 Founded in about 1250, the Swedish capital, Stockholm, is sometimes known as the 'Venice of the North'.

Inari

HAMMERFEST

FINLAND

KUOPIO

OULU

LULEÅ

Gulf of Bothnia

VAASA

LAPLAND

TROMSØ

KIRUNA

NARVIK

UMEÅ

ÖSTERSUND

Lofoten Is.

TRONDHEIM

NORWEGIAN SEA

ICELAND

AKUREYRI

Vatnajökull

REYKJAVÍK

Scale

0   150 km

4 More than a thousand years ago Vikings began to leave their native Scandinavia in search of new lands. They found their way to Britain, Greenland, Newfound-land, Russia and the Mediterranean. This sculpture shows us what a Viking warrior looked like.

6 Legoland in Denmark is an amazing exhibition of sculptures and buildings, all made of plastic bricks. This is a model of the town of Ålborg.

LAHTI
HELSINKI
TURKU
Gulf of Finland
TALLINN
L. Peipus
ESTONIA
RIGA
LATVIA
LITHUANIA
KAUNAS
VILNIUS
Saaremaa
Åland Is.
UPPSALA
STOCKHOLM
LIEPAJA
Gotland
VISBY
Öland
NORRKÖPING
KARLSTAD
Vättern
KARLSKRONA
BALTIC SEA
Vänern
GÖTEBORG
OSLO
COPENHAGEN
MALMÖ
Bornholm
BERGEN
STAVANGER
KRISTIANSAND
Skagerrak
ÅLBORG
ÅRHUS
DENMARK
ODENSE
N

5 In Norway arms of the sea, called fjords, reach deep inland. Norway has such a jagged coastline that if it were straightened out it would reach halfway round the world!

The best farmland in Scandinavia is found in Denmark and the southern tip of Sweden. Cattle, pigs and poultry are raised and cereal crops grown. Fishing is vitally important to the Icelanders and Norwegians, while timber is a big industry, especially in Sweden and Finland. The steel industry in Sweden produces machinery, tools, aircraft and cars.

Across the Baltic Sea lie the small countries of Estonia, Latvia and Lithuania. All regained their independence from the former Soviet Union in 1991, 51 years after being invaded during World War II.

BRITISH ISLES

THE BRITISH ISLES is the name given to all the islands that lie off the north-western coast of Europe, including the two large islands of Great Britain (called 'Great' to distinguish it from 'Little Britain' or Brittany in France) and Ireland.

The United Kingdom consists of the island of Great Britain, which includes England, Scotland and Wales, and Northern Ireland. Most of Britain's uplands are in the north and west, while central and southern regions are mostly low-lying, a dense mix of farmland, towns and cities.

Most of today's Britons are descendants from the many peoples who have settled or invaded the islands in the past: Celts, Romans, Anglo-Saxons, Norsemen and Normans. More recent settlers have come from Asia, Africa and the Caribbean.

The sea has always been important to Britain. There is still a major fishing industry. Since the early days of ocean exploration, sailors travelled to distant parts of the world, closely followed by traders and settlers, who built up a vast empire.

1 Completed in 1779, the Iron Bridge in Coalbrookdale, England, was the world's first bridge made of iron.

2 The western coastline of Scotland is a landscape of sea lochs overlooked by rounded mountains.

3 Cricket (below), England's popular summer sport

8 Little Moreton Hall, built using richly-carved wood, looks like a fairy-tale cottage.

7 The Giant's Causeway, an extraordinary rock formation on the Northern Irish coast.

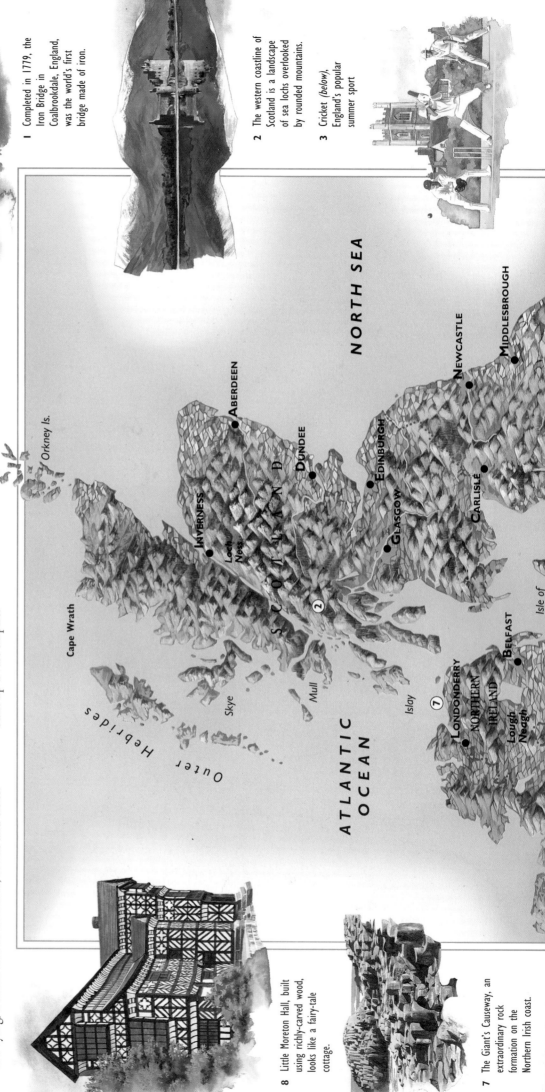

Shetland Is.

Orkney Is.

Cape Wrath

Outer Hebrides

Skye

Mull

Islay

ATLANTIC OCEAN

NORTH SEA

INVERNESS

Loch Ness

ABERDEEN

DUNDEE

EDINBURGH

GLASGOW

CARLISLE

NEWCASTLE

MIDDLESBROUGH

SCOTLAND

LONDONDERRY

NORTHERN IRELAND

BELFAST

Lough Neagh

Isle of

2

7

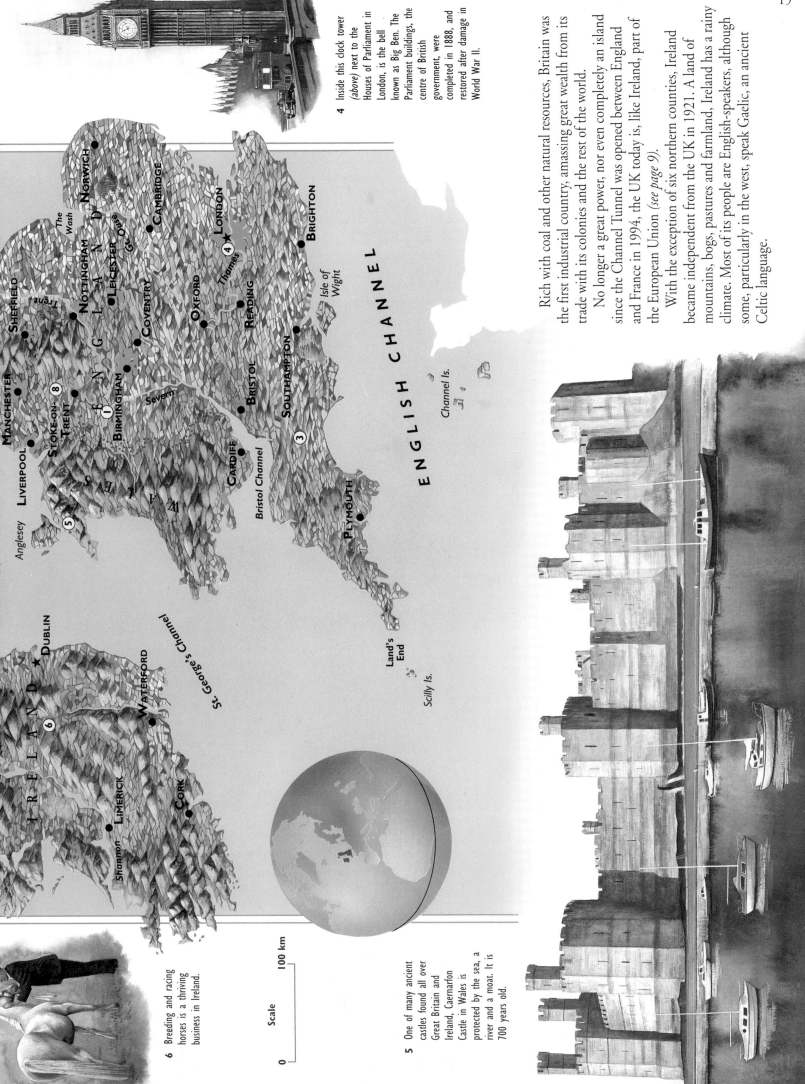

15

4 Inside this clock tower *(above)* next to the Houses of Parliament in London, is the bell known as Big Ben. The Parliament buildings, the centre of British government, were completed in 1888, and restored after damage in World War II.

Rich with coal and other natural resources, Britain was the first industrial country, amassing great wealth from its trade with its colonies and the rest of the world.

No longer a great power, nor even completely an island since the Channel Tunnel was opened between England and France in 1994, the UK today is, like Ireland, part of the European Union *(see page 9)*.

With the exception of six northern counties, Ireland became independent from the UK in 1921. A land of mountains, bogs, pastures and farmland, Ireland has a rainy climate. Most of its people are English-speakers, although some, particularly in the west, speak Gaelic, an ancient Celtic language.

6 Breeding and racing horses is a thriving business in Ireland.

Scale

0 — 100 km

5 One of many ancient castles found all over Great Britain and Ireland, Caernarfon Castle in Wales is protected by the sea, a river and a moat. It is 700 years old.

ENGLISH CHANNEL

IRISH SEA

IRELAND
DUBLIN
WATERFORD
LIMERICK
Shannon
CORK
St George's Channel

ENGLAND
NORWICH
The Wash
CAMBRIDGE
LEICESTER
Gt Ouse
NOTTINGHAM
SHEFFIELD
Trent
MANCHESTER
LIVERPOOL
STOKE-ON-TRENT
BIRMINGHAM
COVENTRY
OXFORD
LONDON
Thames
READING
BRIGHTON
Isle of Wight
SOUTHAMPTON
BRISTOL
Severn
CARDIFF
Bristol Channel
Anglesey
WALES
PLYMOUTH
Land's End
Scilly Is.
Channel Is.

FRANCE

FRANCE is Europe's largest country after Russia and Ukraine. Except in the north-east, where the Flanders plain and Ardennes hills cross into Belgium, it has natural borders on all sides: the sea in the north, west and south, high mountain ranges in the south-west and south-east, and the River Rhine in the east. Nearly every type of landscape in western Europe can be found in France: there are snowy peaks, wide open fields, thick forests, flat marshes and rugged coasts. All over the country there are many

7 France's high-speed train, the TGV

regions each with its own name and different character.

Apart from the hills of Brittany, most of northern and western France is fairly flat. This rich agricultural land is crossed by the Seine, Loire and Garonne rivers and their tributaries. Central, eastern and southern France are mostly hill or mountain, making up about one-third of France's land

6 The abbey of Mont-Saint-Michel stands on an old hill just off the Normandy coast. At high tide, the road leading to it is covered by the sea.

1 In the region of Périgord, the traditional way to hunt for truffles, a kind of mushroom, is to use the keen nose of a trained pig!

Scale
0   100 km

BAY OF BISCAY

CALA

LE HAVRE

AMIEN

ROUEN

PARIS

NORMANDY

BREST

BRITTANY

6

RENNES

LE MANS

7

ORLÉAN

TOURS

Loire

Cher

NANTES

POITIERS

Vienne

LA ROCHELLE

LIMOGES

1

BORDEAUX

Dordogne

2

Lot

GASCONY

Ta

5

BIARRITZ

TOULOUS

Garonne

Pyrenees

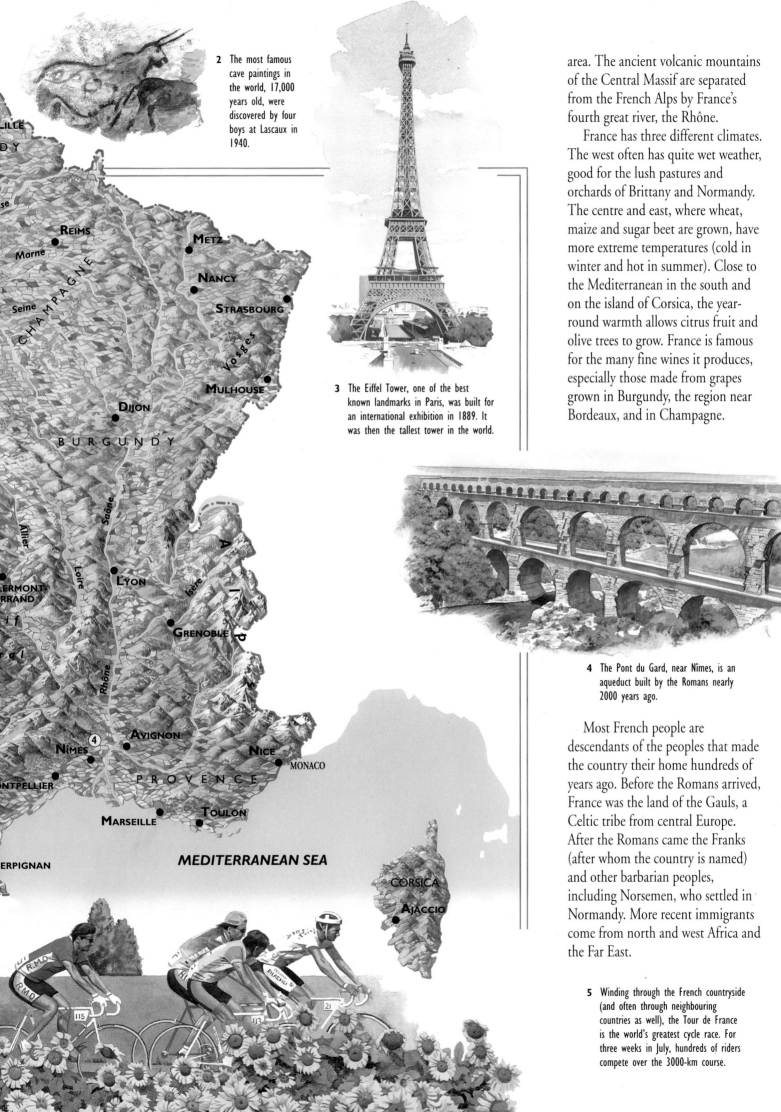

2 The most famous cave paintings in the world, 17,000 years old, were discovered by four boys at Lascaux in 1940.

3 The Eiffel Tower, one of the best known landmarks in Paris, was built for an international exhibition in 1889. It was then the tallest tower in the world.

area. The ancient volcanic mountains of the Central Massif are separated from the French Alps by France's fourth great river, the Rhône.

France has three different climates. The west often has quite wet weather, good for the lush pastures and orchards of Brittany and Normandy. The centre and east, where wheat, maize and sugar beet are grown, have more extreme temperatures (cold in winter and hot in summer). Close to the Mediterranean in the south and on the island of Corsica, the year-round warmth allows citrus fruit and olive trees to grow. France is famous for the many fine wines it produces, especially those made from grapes grown in Burgundy, the region near Bordeaux, and in Champagne.

4 The Pont du Gard, near Nîmes, is an aqueduct built by the Romans nearly 2000 years ago.

Most French people are descendants of the peoples that made the country their home hundreds of years ago. Before the Romans arrived, France was the land of the Gauls, a Celtic tribe from central Europe. After the Romans came the Franks (after whom the country is named) and other barbarian peoples, including Norsemen, who settled in Normandy. More recent immigrants come from north and west Africa and the Far East.

5 Winding through the French countryside (and often through neighbouring countries as well), the Tour de France is the world's greatest cycle race. For three weeks in July, hundreds of riders compete over the 3000-km course.

MEDITERRANEAN SEA

The Netherlands

O NE THIRD of the Netherlands (the name means 'low-lying lands') lies below sea level. Nearly all the remaining land is low and flat. Some areas, called polderlands, were once actually covered by water and have been 'reclaimed' for use as farmland. Behind the low wall of sand-dunes which runs along the west coast and the Frisian Islands, the Dutch built dykes (earth embankments) and dug drainage ditches. Windmills pumped water away along canals, leaving dry, fertile land.

For centuries, the Dutch have fought to protect their land from the sea. Flooding is a constant threat: the sea has sometimes broken through the defences, making thousands homeless. Great barriers between Wadden Sea and IJsselmeer and the arms of the Rhine-Maas Delta were built as further protection.

The Netherlands, sometimes known as Holland (although this name really refers only to one part of the country), is one of the most densely populated countries in the world. In between the farmland and famous bulbfields, large industrial cities have grown up.

1 Until the nineteenth century, windmills like this one *(above)* were used to pump water out of the drainage ditches into canals.

2 Skinny Bridge crosses an Amsterdam canal *(above)*.

3 Men in traditional dress carry cheeses at the market in Alkmaar *(below)*.

8 Rotterdam, situated near the mouth of the Rhine, is the busiest port in the world. Goods from Germany's industrial cities are carried downstream to Rotterdam by barge.

7 The sea is important to the Dutch. They have fought to win land from

NORTH SEA

NETHERLANDS

GRONINGEN

LEEUWARDEN

ENSCHEDE

ZWOLLE

APELDOORN

ARNHEM

NIJMEGEN

Maas

Frisian Islands

Wadden Sea

IJsselmeer

DEN HELDER

ALKMAAR ③

HAARLEM

AMSTERDAM ②

UTRECHT

Lek

Waal

THE HAGUE

LEIDEN

ROTTERDAM ⑧

DORDRECHT ①

TILBURG

BREDA

EINDHOVEN

⑦

Rhine-Maas Delta

BELGIUM AND LUXEMBOURG

BELGIUM is a country of two halves. In the north, on the plain of Flanders, the countryside is a patchwork of farmland criss-crossed by canals. The people, known as Flemings, speak the language of their neighbours, Dutch, or Flemish as it is known here. In the south, beyond the Meuse and Sambre rivers lie the forested slopes and deep valleys of the Ardennes hills. Here, apart from a small German-speaking region close to the eastern border, live the Walloons, the French-speaking Belgians. Both French and Flemish are spoken in the capital Brussels, the centre of government for the European Union.

The Grand Duchy of Luxembourg is a small country on the southern slopes of the Ardennes. Most Luxembourgers speak German, or their own dialect of it called Letzeburgesch.

4 The castle of Vianden in the wooded hills of Luxembourg

Scale

0   60 km

5 Founded on the Flemish wool and cloth industry, Ghent and Bruges (*below*) were great medieval cities. Laced with canals, Bruges (its Flemish name is Brugge) still has many old buildings.

6 The Atomium is a museum of science in Brussels.

it, they have sailed across it to build a great trading empire, and they have used it as a source of food. Fishing vessels (*above*) make catches in the rich North Sea fishing grounds.

OOSTENDE · GHENT · Scheldt · BRUSSELS · MONS · CHARLEROI · Sambre · NAMUR · Meuse · LIÈGE · MAASTRICHT · FLANDERS · BELGIUM · WALLONIA · Ardennes · LUXEMBOURG

PORTUGAL

SITUATED on the western coast of the Iberian peninsula, Portugal has long held close ties with the sea. More than 500 years ago, Portuguese sailors set off round the coast of Africa to open trade routes to the East. They founded colonies in Africa, Asia and South America. Their empire has disappeared, but more than 100 million people still speak Portuguese.

Portugal is one of Western Europe's poorest countries. Many people work on the farms or in the

6 The Luiz I bridge spans the River Douro at Porto, Portugal.

fishing industry. Shellfish, anchovies and sardines are caught in the coastal waters. Portugal produces most of the world's cork, stripped from the bark of a kind of oak tree, the Cork Oak. Vines grow in the river valleys of northern and central Portugal. Some of the grapes are used for making port, a sweet wine which is the speciality of the region near Porto.

Like Spain, Portugal is drier in the south. Here, in the Algarve, tourism has become an important industry.

5 La Mancha is the name given to the plains lying south-east of Madrid. It is famous as the place where Don Quixote, the legendary knight, attacked the windmills *(right)* he took to be giants.

1 A traditional fishing boat *(left)*, called a *moliceiro*, sails off the Portuguese coast.

2 This old woman *(right)* comes from a small Portuguese village.

LA CORUÑA · SANTANDER · BILBA

GALICIA

Sil · LEÓN · OLD CASTILE · BURG

VIGO

ATLANTIC OCEAN

VALLADOLID · Duero

⑥ PORTO · Douro

SALAMANCA

① S · P · A

COIMBRA · ③ MADRID ★

NEW CASTI

Tagus · TOLEDO

Guadiana

② CIUDAD REAL ⑤

LISBON ★ · BADAJOZ

CÓRDOBA Guadalquivir

ALGARVE · ANDALUCIA

SEVILLA

GRANADA ④

Sierra Neva

CÁDIZ · MÁLAGA

GIBRALTAR (Br.)

3 El Escorial *(right)* dates from the 16th century, when Spain ruled much of Europe and America. The monastery was used as a royal residence by the emperor Philip II.

SPAIN

S PAIN stands at the crossroads between Europe and Africa. Celts, Greeks, Carthaginians, Romans, Visigoths and Moors have all invaded the country. In turn, Spain conquered vast parts of the Americas and was once the most powerful nation in the world.

The Pyrenees mountains mark Spain's border with the rest of Europe. Northern Spain has most of the country's industrial cities. The peoples of Galicia, Catalonia and the Basque

SAN SEBASTIÁN

BASQUE PROVINCES

Pyrenees

ANDORRA

ARAGON

ZARAGOZA   Ebro   LÉRIDA

CATALONIA

BARCELONA

Scale
0   100 km

Menorca

Mallorca

CUENCA

PALMA

VALENCIA

Júcar

ncha

Ibiza

ALBACETE

ALICANTE

MURCIA

MEDITERRANEAN SEA

CARTAGENA

N

4 The Alhambra of Granada was built by Moorish kings 600 years ago. This is the Court of Lions.

Provinces speak their own languages.

Farther south, across vineyards, wheat-fields and olive groves, the climate becomes drier. There are small mountain ranges but the land is mostly high and flat. In the centre of Spain lies the capital, Madrid.

Parts of southern Spain are dry scrubland grazed only by sheep and goats. Andalucia is famous for many things: fighting bulls, sherry, orange trees, village festivals or *fiestas*, flamenco dancers and Moorish castles. Tourist beaches and hotels line the Mediterranean coast.

GERMANY

EUROPE'S second largest country by population, Germany is one of the richest industrial countries in the world. Cars, chemicals, steel and electronic goods are produced in its many large cities. The Ruhr Valley cities in the west of the country have grown so large they have merged with one another.

Germany became a single nation for the first time in 1871. Before then, Germans lived in a land made up of a mixture of small duchies, principalities and kingdoms.

Divided into East and West after World War II in 1945, Germany became united again in 1990 when the countries of Eastern Europe, including East Germany threw out their Communist governments.

Northern Germany forms part of the North European Plain, which stretches from the North Sea to the Ural Mountains in Russia. Wooded uplands, the remains of ancient mountain ranges, rise in central and southern Germany. Germany's border with Austria runs along the northern slopes of the Alps.

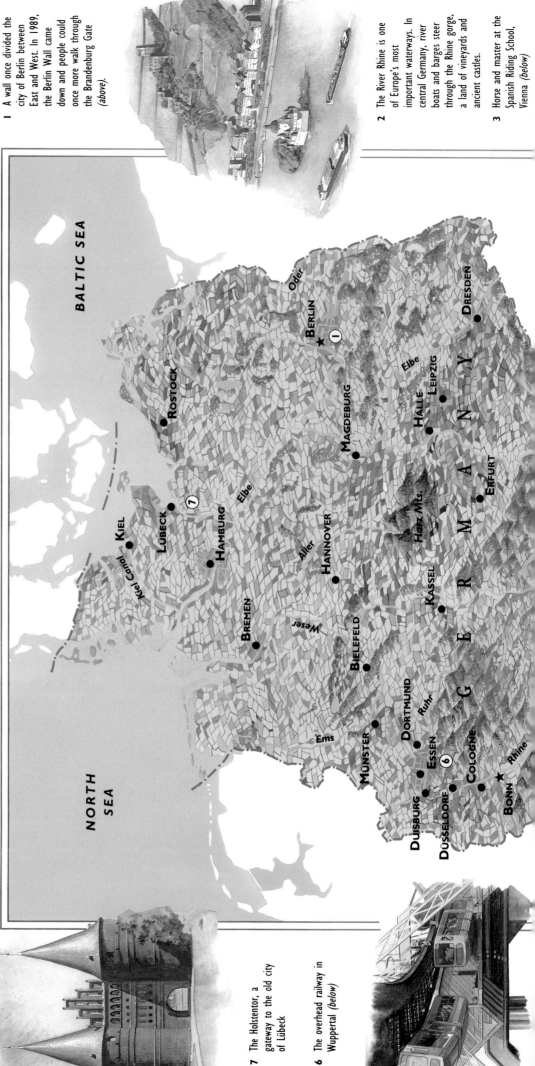

1 A wall once divided the city of Berlin between East and West. In 1989, the Berlin Wall came down and people could once more walk through the Brandenburg Gate *(above)*.

2 The River Rhine is one of Europe's most important waterways. In central Germany, river boats and barges steer through the Rhine gorge, a land of vineyards and ancient castles.

3 Horse and master at the Spanish Riding School, Vienna *(below)*.

7 The Holstentor, a gateway to the old city of Lübeck

6 The overhead railway in Wuppertal *(below)*

BALTIC SEA

NORTH SEA

GERMANY

Berlin, Rostock, Kiel, Lübeck, Hamburg, Bremen, Hannover, Magdeburg, Halle, Leipzig, Dresden, Erfurt, Kassel, Bielefeld, Münster, Dortmund, Essen, Duisburg, Düsseldorf, Cologne, Bonn

Oder, Elbe, Aller, Weser, Ems, Ruhr, Rhine, Harz Mts., Kiel Canal

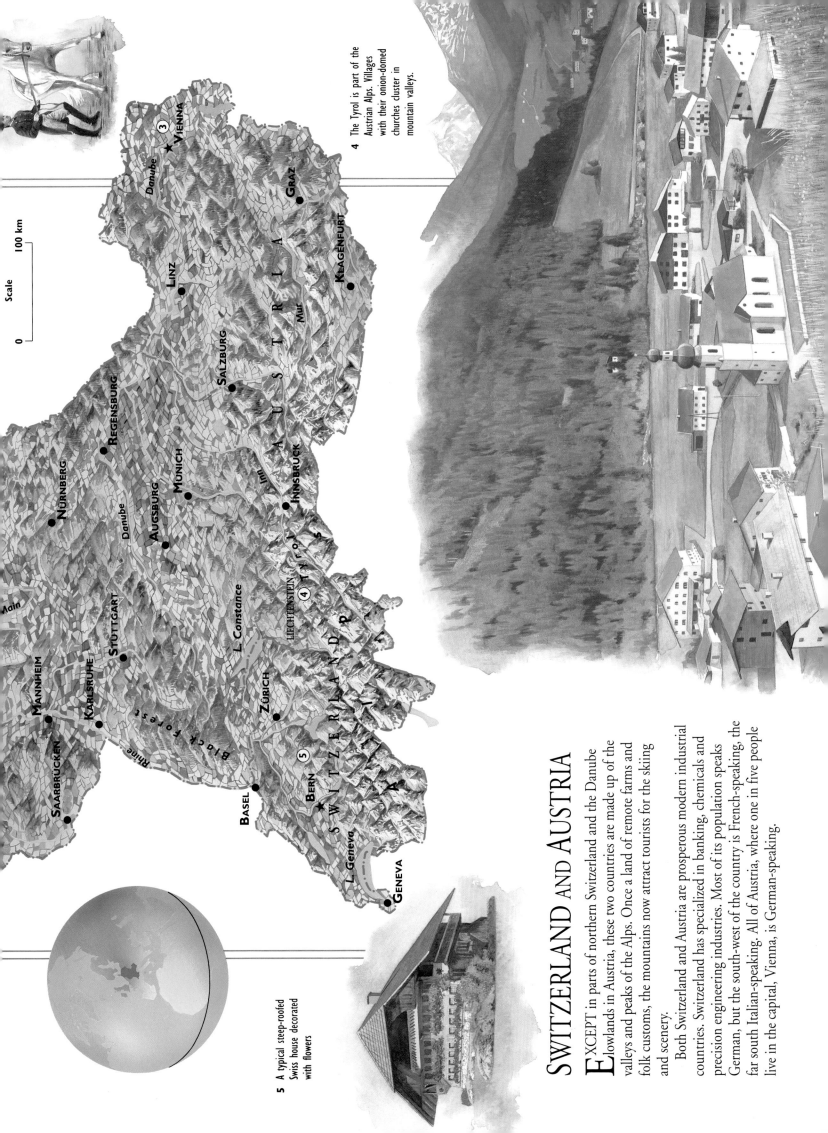

Scale

0   100 km

MANNHEIM
SAARBRÜCKEN
KARLSRUHE
STUTTGART
Main
Rhine
Black Forest
NÜRNBERG
REGENSBURG
Danube
AUGSBURG
MUNICH
LINZ
Danube
③ VIENNA
GRAZ
Mur
SALZBURG
Inn
INNSBRUCK
④ T y r o l
A U S T R I A
KLAGENFURT
LIECHTENSTEIN
L. Constance
ZÜRICH
⑤ BERN
BASEL
S W I T Z E R L A N D
L. Geneva
GENEVA
L. Geneva

4 The Tyrol is part of the Austrian Alps. Villages with their onion-domed churches cluster in mountain valleys.

5 A typical steep-roofed Swiss house decorated with flowers

SWITZERLAND AND AUSTRIA

EXCEPT in parts of northern Switzerland and the Danube lowlands in Austria, these two countries are made up of the valleys and peaks of the Alps. Once a land of remote farms and folk customs, the mountains now attract tourists for the skiing and scenery.

Both Switzerland and Austria are prosperous modern industrial countries. Switzerland has specialized in banking, chemicals and precision engineering industries. Most of its population speaks German, but the south-west of the country is French-speaking, the far south Italian-speaking. All of Austria, where one in five people live in the capital, Vienna, is German-speaking.

ITALY

SHAPED RATHER LIKE A BOOT, Italy is a long peninsula surrounded on three sides by the waters of the Mediterranean Sea. Rimmed around its top end are the high snow-capped mountains of the Alps. South-flowing rivers meet the Po in a wide, flat plain which opens out to the Adriatic Sea.

Running down the length of the boot to the toe are the Apennines. These mountains are thickly wooded. Farther south, there are smaller trees and bushes called scrub. Both

Sicily and Sardinia are rugged, hilly islands. Italy has three famous active volcanoes: Vesuvius, Stromboli and Etna.

Italy's regions united to become a single country in 1871. From one part of the nation to another there are great differences in the way of life. In the north, there are rich, industrial cities, vine-covered mountain slopes and fertile fields of wheat, maize and tomatoes. The south, Sicily and Sardinia, are not so rich: many people have left to work in the north.

1 The beautiful city of Venice was built on small islands off the Adriatic coast. Its 'streets' are canals with gondolas (above) and water buses as its traffic.

2 The Dolomites (above) form part of the Alps. These jagged mountains are made of limestone.

3 A cardinal (below), a senior figure in the Roman Catholic Church in Vatican City State

Scale

0   100 km

ADRIATIC SEA

TRIESTE
BOLZANO
VENICE
VERONA
PADOVA
BOLOGNA
SAN MARINO
ANCONA
PESCARA
PERUGIA
TERNI
Tiber
ROME
VATICAN CITY STATE
PARMA
FLORENCE
Arno
LA SPEZIA
LIVORNO
Elba
GENOA
BRESCIA
MILAN
Adda
Adige
Po
A p e n n i n e s
A l p s
TURIN
Po

8 A wolf from the Abruzzi National Park in the Apennines

7 Soccer is a very popular sport in Italy. Huge crowds attend matches held in all the big cities.

4 Vesuvius erupted in 79 AD, burying the Roman town of Pompeii in ash. The remains of a great civilization have since been uncovered for all to see.

MALTA

The islands of Malta lie in the Mediterranean Sea between Sicily and Africa. The Maltese speak a language related to Arabic. Malta has many natural harbours, prized by the empires that have possessed the islands. Independent from Britain since 1964, it is one of the most densely populated countries in the world.

VATICAN CITY STATE

The Vatican is the smallest independent country in the world. It lies on a hill west of the Tiber river within the city of Rome, Italy's capital. It is home to the Pope, the head of the Roman Catholic Church.

TYRRHENIAN SEA

MEDITERRANEAN SEA

BARI

⑥ BRINDISI

TARANTO

Vesuvius

SALERNO

④

NAPLES

REGGIO DI CALABRIA

MESSINA

Etna

CATANIA

Stromboli

PALERMO

S I C I L Y

VALLETTA

MALTA

Pantelleria

SASSARI

S A R D I N I A

CAGLIARI

6 These houses in Alberobello in Apulia, the 'heel' of Italy, are shaped like pepperpots. Their roofs are made of stone slabs.

5 San Gimignano is a small town in Tuscany, central Italy. Fifteen towers survive out of 72 that were built more than 600 years ago.

EASTERN EUROPE

OVER THE YEARS, the boundaries between the countries of Eastern Europe have been redrawn many times. Most recently, the two former Soviet Republics of Ukraine and Belarus have come into being, while Czechoslovakia has divided in two. Earlier in the century, what is now Polish territory was split between Germany and Russia; Czechoslovakia and Hungary were part of the Austro-Hungarian Empire. Slav and

7 A couple at a Slovak wedding wear traditional dress.

Hungarian peoples have lived in these lands for many years.

North of the Sudetes and Carpathian Mountains, the North European Plain fans out across Poland, Belarus and Ukraine. Forests remain in some parts but elsewhere the land is given over to farming. Fields of wheat, barley, sugar beet and sunflowers cover the lowlands of Ukraine, once known as the 'bread basket' of the Soviet Union. Potatoes,

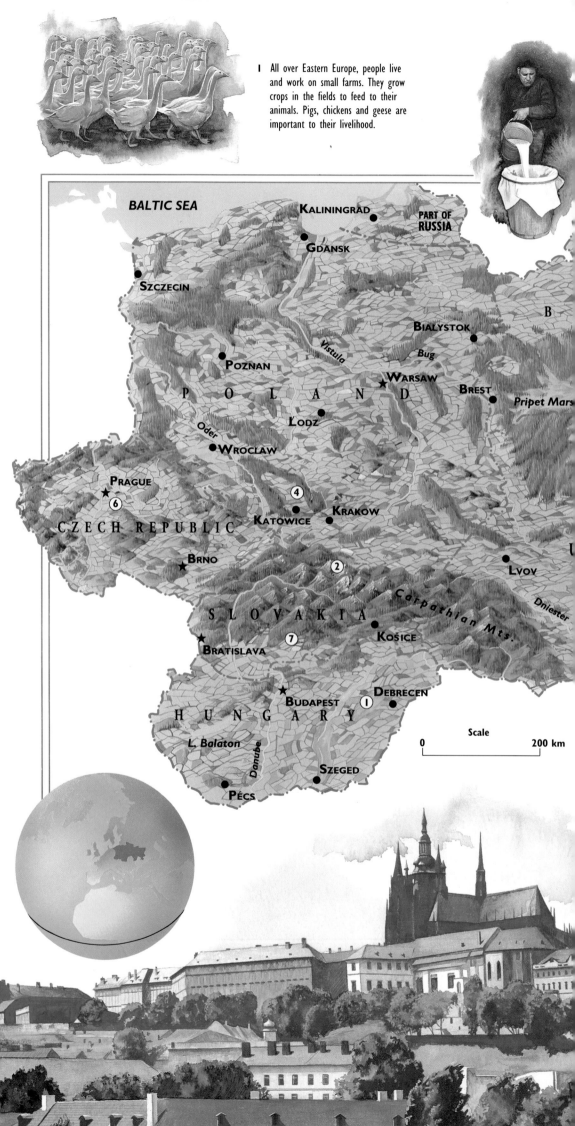

1 All over Eastern Europe, people live and work on small farms. They grow crops in the fields to feed to their animals. Pigs, chickens and geese are important to their livelihood.

BALTIC SEA

KALININGRAD

PART OF RUSSIA

GDANSK

SZCZECIN

BIAŁYSTOK

Vistula

Bug

POZNAN

WARSAW

P O L A N D

BREST

Pripet Mars

Oder

ŁODZ

WROCLAW

PRAGUE
⑥

④

CZECH REPUBLIC

KATOWICE

KRAKOW

BRNO

②

LVOV

Carpathian Mts.

S L O V A K I A

Dniester

KOŠICE

⑦

BRATISLAVA

BUDAPEST

DEBRECEN
①

H U N G A R Y

Scale

0   200 km

L. Balaton

Danube

SZEGED

PÉCS

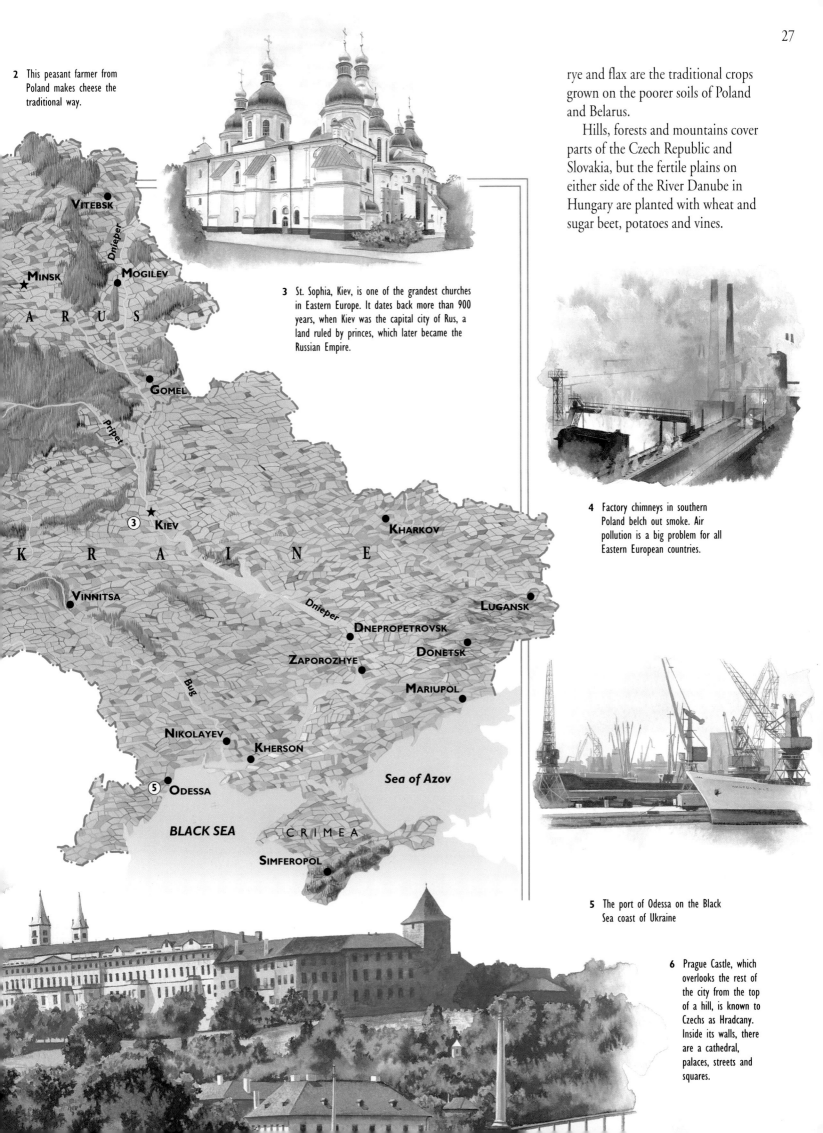

2 This peasant farmer from Poland makes cheese the traditional way.

3 St. Sophia, Kiev, is one of the grandest churches in Eastern Europe. It dates back more than 900 years, when Kiev was the capital city of Rus, a land ruled by princes, which later became the Russian Empire.

rye and flax are the traditional crops grown on the poorer soils of Poland and Belarus.

Hills, forests and mountains cover parts of the Czech Republic and Slovakia, but the fertile plains on either side of the River Danube in Hungary are planted with wheat and sugar beet, potatoes and vines.

4 Factory chimneys in southern Poland belch out smoke. Air pollution is a big problem for all Eastern European countries.

5 The port of Odessa on the Black Sea coast of Ukraine

6 Prague Castle, which overlooks the rest of the city from the top of a hill, is known to Czechs as Hradcany. Inside its walls, there are a cathedral, palaces, streets and squares.

VITEBSK

Dnieper

MINSK

MOGILEV

B A R U S

GOMEL

Pripet

③ KIEV

K R A I N E

KHARKOV

VINNITSA

Dnieper

LUGANSK

DNEPROPETROVSK

ZAPOROZHYE

DONETSK

MARIUPOL

Bug

NIKOLAYEV

KHERSON

⑤ ODESSA

Sea of Azov

BLACK SEA

C R I M E A

SIMFEROPOL

THE BALKANS

THE COUNTRIES of south-east Europe lying between the Adriatic Sea and the Black Sea are known as the Balkan states. Mountains run the length of the western Balkans, from the Alps to southern Greece, and in a curve through Romania in the north. Where the two ranges meet, the River Danube courses through a deep gorge known as the Iron Gate.

The Danube lowlands in Serbia, Romania and Bulgaria are the best farming areas where wheat and maize are grown. Elsewhere, the uplands are grazed by sheep and goats, though vines, fruit and olive trees grow on some sunny fertile slopes.

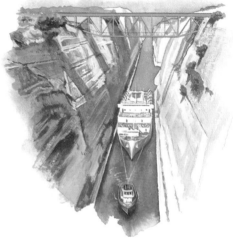

7 The Corinth Canal was cut across a narrow strip of land 5 km long in 1893.

GREECE

ONE FIFTH of Greece's total land area is made up of islands. Even on the mainland, nowhere is more than 80 kilometres from the sea. Most of Greece is covered by rugged mountains, so people have made use of the sea, both as a source of food and a means to travel between places. In the days of classical Greece, from around 800 years before Christ, Greek art, literature and ideas flourished as part of a great civilization. Today, Greece is a member of the European Union and a popular holiday destination for tourists.

I Farm buildings in Slovenia have a wooden frame called a *kozolec* used for storing and drying hay.

SLOVENIA
LJUBLJANA ①
ZAGREB
RIJEKA
CROATIA
Sava
BOSNIA
SPLIT
SARAJEVO
BELGRADE
SERBIA
MONTE-NEGRO
NIŠ
SOFIA ③
BULGARIA
SKOPJE
MACEDONIA
PLOVDIV
TIRANE
ALBANIA
THESSALONIKI
Corfu
GREECE
AEGEAN SEA
Limnos
Lesbos
Kefallinia
Khios
ATHENS ⑥
PATRAI ⑦
Naxos
IZMIR
MEDITERRANEAN SEA
Crete
Karpathos
Rhode

ADRIATIC SEA

CLUJ-NAPOCA
IAŞI
MOLDOV
KISH
TIMISOARA
ROMANIA
Carpathian Mts. ②
Iron Gate
BUCHAREST
Danube
CONSTAN
VARNA
Bosp
ISTANBUL
BURSA

2 A Romanian shepherd from the Carpathian Mountains in traditional dress

3 The Alexander Nevski Cathedral in Sofia, capital city of Bulgaria. Alexander Nevski was a Russian prince and Slav hero who lived in the Middle Ages.

Scale

0   200 km

TURKEY

ANATOLIA, a peninsula lying between the Black Sea and the Mediterranean Sea, together with a small corner of Europe just the other side of the Bosporus, are all that now remain today of the Turkish empire. It

4 This is a whirling dervish, a Muslim worshipper from Turkey who performs an energetic dance.

once stretched from Iran in the east almost as far as Vienna in the west.

Turkey is a mountainous country. Inland, the high plains and ranges are mostly dry, although wheat is grown

BLACK SEA

SAMSUN

ERZURUM

ANKARA

Kizilirmak

U R K E Y

L. Van

ESKIŞEHIR

KAYSERI

DIYARBAKIR

Tigris

L. Tuz

4

KONYA

Euphrates

GAZIANTEP

ADANA

ANTALYA

6 The Acropolis, overlooking the Greek capital city of Athens, was built 2500 years ago. From the steps of the temples, of which the most famous is the Parthenon, on the right, it was possible to see if enemy ships were approaching the coast.

CYPRUS

NICOSIA

5 People still live in these ancient cave-houses in Cappadocia, Turkey.

in some parts, and forests cover the mountain slopes. In valleys and lowlands close to the Mediterranean coast, tobacco, figs, sultanas and cotton are the main crops. About half of all Turks still work in the fields, many on small hill farms with just a few sheep and goats.

The Turkish people, almost all Muslims, are descended from peoples who came from Russia and Mongolia. There are still Turkish-speaking peoples in these places, as well as in the new Central Asian republics.

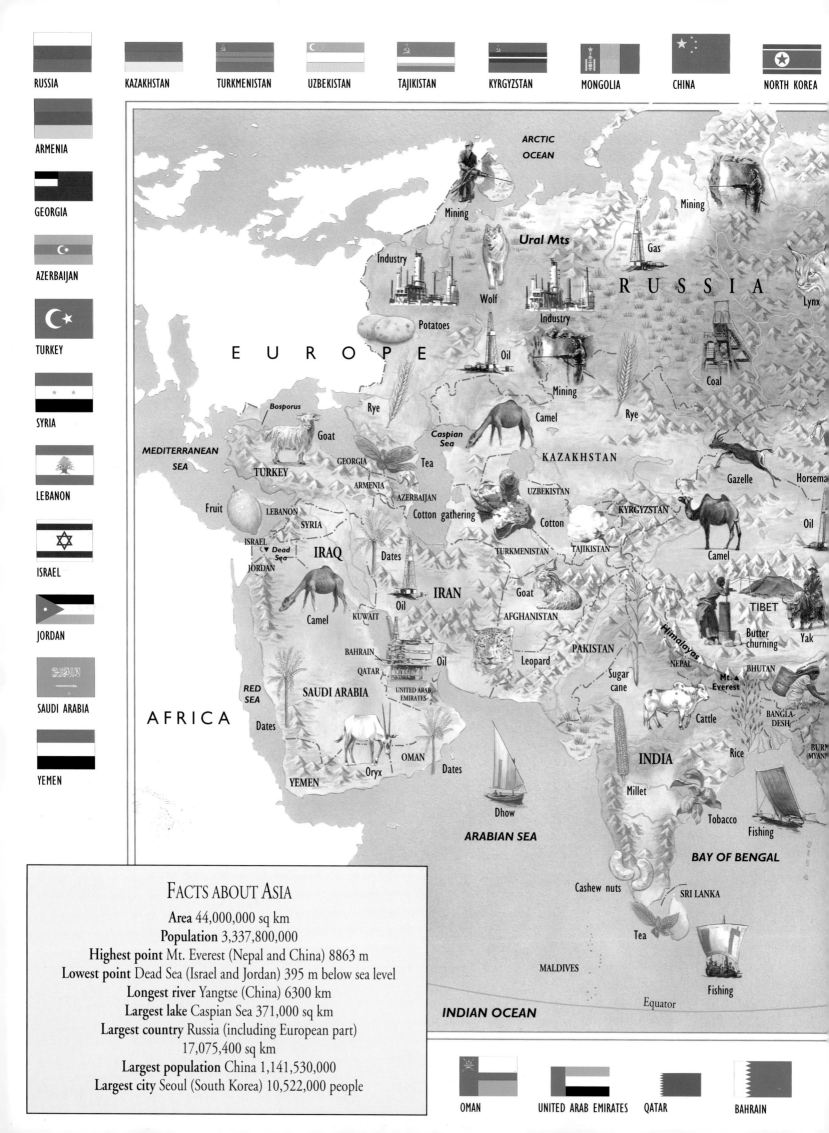

RUSSIA
KAZAKHSTAN
TURKMENISTAN
UZBEKISTAN
TAJIKISTAN
KYRGYZSTAN
MONGOLIA
CHINA
NORTH KOREA

ARMENIA

GEORGIA

AZERBAIJAN

TURKEY

SYRIA

LEBANON

ISRAEL

JORDAN

SAUDI ARABIA

YEMEN

ARCTIC OCEAN

Mining

Ural Mts

Industry

Wolf

Mining

Gas

R U S S I A

Lynx

E U R O P E

Potatoes

Industry

Oil

Coal

Mining

Rye

Camel

Rye

Bosporus

Caspian Sea

KAZAKHSTAN

MEDITERRANEAN SEA

Goat

Gazelle

Horsema

Goat

GEORGIA

Tea

UZBEKISTAN

KYRGYZSTAN

ARMENIA

AZERBAIJAN

Cotton gathering

Cotton

TURKEY

Camel

Fruit

TURKMENISTAN

TAJIKISTAN

LEBANON

Oil

SYRIA

Camel

ISRAEL

▼ *Dead Sea*

IRAQ

Dates

Goat

TIBET

JORDAN

Oil

IRAN

AFGHANISTAN

Butter churning

Yak

Camel

KUWAIT

Leopard

PAKISTAN

NEPAL

BHUTAN

BAHRAIN

Sugar cane

Mt. ▲ Everest

QATAR

Oil

BANGLA-DESH

RED SEA

SAUDI ARABIA

UNITED ARAB EMIRATES

Cattle

AFRICA

Dates

Rice

BURM (MYANN

OMAN

INDIA

Oryx

Dates

Millet

YEMEN

Tobacco

Fishing

Dhow

Cashew nuts

SRI LANKA

ARABIAN SEA

BAY OF BENGAL

Tea

MALDIVES

Fishing

Equator

INDIAN OCEAN

FACTS ABOUT ASIA

Area 44,000,000 sq km
Population 3,337,800,000
Highest point Mt. Everest (Nepal and China) 8863 m
Lowest point Dead Sea (Israel and Jordan) 395 m below sea level
Longest river Yangtse (China) 6300 km
Largest lake Caspian Sea 371,000 sq km
Largest country Russia (including European part)
17,075,400 sq km
Largest population China 1,141,530,000
Largest city Seoul (South Korea) 10,522,000 people

OMAN
UNITED ARAB EMIRATES
QATAR
BAHRAIN

ASIA

REACHING NEARLY HALFWAY around the globe, Asia is the largest continent of all. The Ural and Caucasus mountains mark the boundaries with Europe to the west. Russia, the world's largest country, lies partly in Asia and partly in Europe. A small part of Turkey north of the Bosporus strait is in Europe.

Siberia, in the far north, borders the icy waters of the Arctic Ocean. Frozen plains, called the tundra, and, farther south, vast coniferous forests are home to reindeer, wolves and other cold-weather wildlife. Few people live in these parts, although coal, gas and other minerals are mined here.

More than half the world's population lives in south and east Asia. Some countries such as South Korea and Singapore have become rich industrial nations. There are large areas of farmland, but forests are cleared to make more room for fields and many kinds of animals are now endangered.

Much of central Asia is desert or grassland, bordered in the south by the great plateau of Tibet and the Himalayas, the highest mountains in the world. To the south-west lies the Middle East, famous for its vast reserves of oil. It is mostly desert, apart from the 'fertile crescent' which stretches from the Persian Gulf to the shores of the Mediterranean.

RICE TERRACES

For three out of every five people in the world, rice is their main food. All over south and east Asia rice is grown as it has been for centuries, in waterlogged fields called paddies. Where the land is hilly, especially in the Philippines and Indonesia, steps or terraces are built into the slopes so that the floodwaters do not flow away.

SOUTH KOREA

JAPAN

TAIWAN

PHILIPPINES

INDONESIA

MALAYSIA

SINGAPORE

 VIETNAM

 CAMBODIA

 LAOS

 THAILAND

 BURMA (MYANMAR)

 BANGLADESH

 BHUTAN

 NEPAL

 INDIA

 SRI LANKA

 MALDIVES

 PAKISTAN

 AFGHANISTAN

 IRAN

KUWAIT

IRAQ

Reindeer

Lemming

Coal

SIBERIA

Seal

Brown bear

Soya beans

Rice harvesting

NORTH KOREA

Sheep

Coal

JAPAN

Mining

SOUTH KOREA

Fruit

MONGOLIA

Fishing

Maize

Industry

CHINA

Yangtse

Pigs

PACIFIC OCEAN

TAIWAN

Tobacco

Giant panda

Rice

Fishing with cormorants

Planting rice

LAOS

THAILAND

Logging

VIETNAM

Junk

PHILIPPINES

CAMBODIA

Oil

Rubber

Copra

Rice

BRUNEI

MALAYSIA

Cloves

Spiny anteater

Tin mining

SINGAPORE

Orang-utan

INDONESIA

Rubber

Planting rice

NATIONS OF ASIA

AFGHANISTAN
Area 652,225 sq km **Population** 15,900,000
Capital Kabul **Languages** Pashto, Dari

ARMENIA
Area 29,800 sq km **Population** 3,305,000
Capital Yerevan **Language** Armenian

AZERBAIJAN
Area 88,600 sq km **Population** 7,021,000
Capital Baku **Language** Azeri

BAHRAIN
Area 691.2 sq km **Population** 412,000
Capital Manama **Language** Arabic

BANGLADESH
Area 143,998 sq km **Pop.** 102,563,000
Capital Dhaka **Languages** Bengali, English

BHUTAN
Area 47,000 sq km **Population** 1,447,000
Capital Thimphu **Language** Dzongkha

BRUNEI
Area 5765 sq km **Population** 226,000
Capital Bandar Seri Begawan
Languages Malay, Chinese

6 Indian girl

BURMA (MYANMAR)
Area 672,552 sq km **Population** 46,300,000
Capital Rangoon **Language** Burmese

CAMBODIA
Area 181,035 sq km **Population** 8,345,000
Capital Phnom Penh **Language** Khmer

CHINA
Area 9,571,300 sq km **Population**
1,141,530,000 **Capital** Beijing
Language Chinese (many dialects)

GEORGIA
Area 69,700 sq km **Population** 5,401,000
Capital Tbilisi **Language** Georgian

HONG KONG
Area 1067 sq km **Population** 5,533,000
Languages Chinese, English

INDIA
Area 3,287,590 sq km **Pop.** 853,400,000
Capital New Delhi **Languages** Hindi, Bengali,
Bihari, Telugu, Marathi, Tamil, English

INDONESIA
Area 1,904,569 sq km **Pop.** 189,400,000
Capital Jakarta **Language** Indonesian

IRAN
Area 1,648,000 sq km **Population** 49,857,384
Capital Tehran **Language** Farsi

IRAQ
Area 438,317 sq km **Population** 16,110,000
Capital Baghdad **Language** Arabic

ISRAEL
Area 21,946 sq km **Population** 4,406,500
Capital Jerusalem **Languages** Hebrew, Arabic

1 Omani boy

KAZAKHSTAN
Area 2,717,300 sq km **Pop.** 16,690,300
Capital Alma-Ata **Languages** Kazakh, Russian

KUWAIT
Area 17,818 sq km **Population** 2,189,000
Capital Kuwait **Language** Arabic

5 Vietnamese boy

JAPAN
Area 377,815 sq km **Pop.** 123,850,000
Capital Tokyo **Language** Japanese

JORDAN
Area 97,740 sq km **Population** 4,100,000
Capital Amman **Language** Arabic

KYRGYZSTAN
Area 198,500 sq km **Population** 4,372,000
Capital Bishkek **Language** Kyrgyz

LAOS
Area 236,800 sq km **Population** 4,218,000
Capital Viangchan **Languages** Lao, French

LEBANON
Area 10,452 sq km **Population** 3,360,000
Capital Beirut **Language** Arabic

MACAO
Area 16 sq km **Population** 462,000

MONGOLIA
Area 1,565,000 sq km **Population** 1,900,000 **Capital** Ulan Bator
Language Kalkha Mongol

NORTH KOREA
Area 120,538 sq km **Population** 21,390,000
Capital Pyongyang **Language** Korean

OMAN
Area 271,950 sq km **Population** 1,334,000
Capital Muscat **Language** Arabic

PAKISTAN
Area 803,943 sq km **Pop.** 114,600,000
Capital Islamabad **Language** Urdu

PHILIPPINES
Area 300,000 sq km **Population** 62,170,000
Capital Manila **Languages** English, Pilipino

QATAR
Area 11,437 sq km **Population** 369,000
Capital Doha **Language** Arabic

RUSSIA
Area 17,075,400 sq km **Pop.** 148,543,000
Capital Moscow **Language** Russian, 38 other languages

SAUDI ARABIA
Area 2,400,900 sq km **Pop.** 13,612,000
Capital Riyadh **Language** Arabic

SINGAPORE
Area 616 sq km **Population** 2,757,000
Languages Chinese, English, Malay, Tamil

SOUTH KOREA
Area 99,222 sq km **Population** 42,082,000
Capital Seoul **Language** Korean

SRI LANKA
Area 64,453 sq km **Population** 17,200,000
Capital Colombo **Languages** Sinhalese, Tamil

SYRIA
Area 185,180 sq km **Population** 12,315,000
Capital Damascus **Language** Arabic

TAIWAN
Area 35,590 sq km **Population** 20,200,000
Capital Taipei **Language** Chinese

TAJIKISTAN
Area 143,100 sq km **Population** 5,112,000
Capital Dushanbe **Language** Tajik

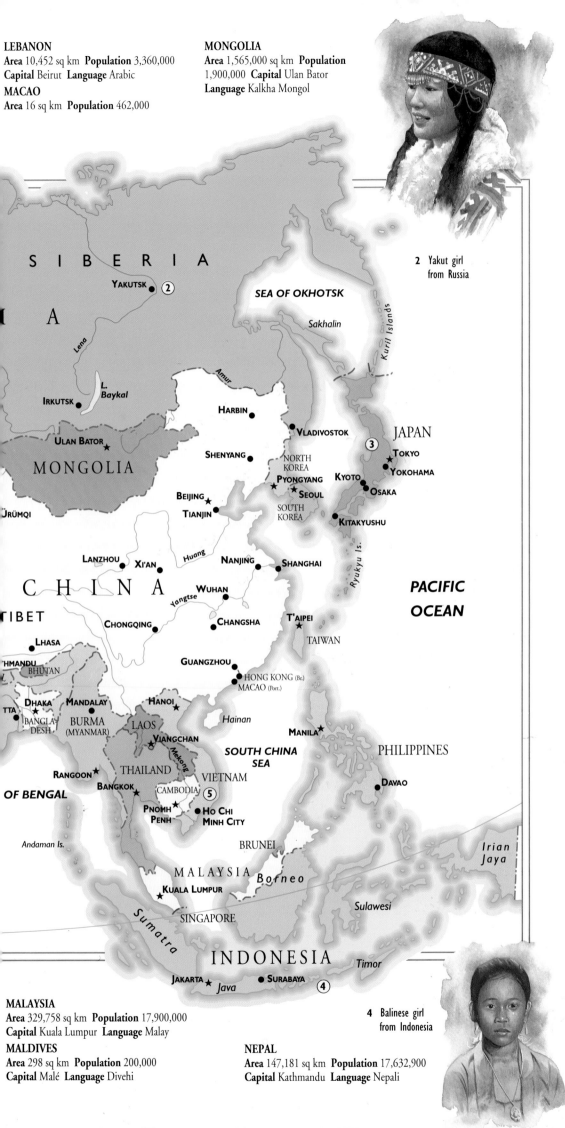

2 Yakut girl from Russia

3 Japanese boy

4 Balinese girl from Indonesia

THAILAND
Area 513,115 sq km **Population** 54,536,000
Capital Bangkok **Language** Thai

TURKEY
Area 779,452 sq km **Population** 63,720,000
Capital Ankara **Language** Turkish

TURKMENISTAN
Area 488,100 sq km **Population** 3,621,700
Capital Ashkhabad **Language** Turkmen

UNITED ARAB EMIRATES
Area 75,150 sq km **Population** 11,384,000
Capital Abu Dhabi **Language** Arabic

UZBEKISTAN
Area 447,400 sq km **Population** 20,322,000
Capital Tashkent **Language** Uzbek

VIETNAM
Area 328,566 sq km **Population** 70,200,000
Capital Hanoi **Languages** Vietnamese, French

YEMEN
Area 477,530 sq km **Population** 11,494,000
Capital San'a **Language** Arabic

MALAYSIA
Area 329,758 sq km **Population** 17,900,000
Capital Kuala Lumpur **Language** Malay

MALDIVES
Area 298 sq km **Population** 200,000
Capital Malé **Language** Divehi

NEPAL
Area 147,181 sq km **Population** 17,632,900
Capital Kathmandu **Language** Nepali

RUSSIA

THE LARGEST COUNTRY in the world, Russia was part of the Soviet Union until that country broke up in 1991. Most of its population live in the European part, west of the Ural Mountains. Its Asian territories to the east stretch to within a few kilometres of Alaska, North America. Besides Slav, around 100 different languages are spoken within its boundaries.

Natural grassland lies between the northern forests   and the desert

6 The Motherland statue, more than 80 metres high, is a monument to a battle in World War II.

scrub of Kazakhstan. Known as the steppes, the black soils are good for the cultivation of wheat, rye, millet and sunflower crops.

Russia became an important industrial country in the twentieth century. It has enormous reserves of coal, oil, gas, iron and other metals.

1 A carpet-maker from Tajikistan

2 Many old buildings in Russia are made of wood. This church was built at Kizhi, an island on Lake Onega.

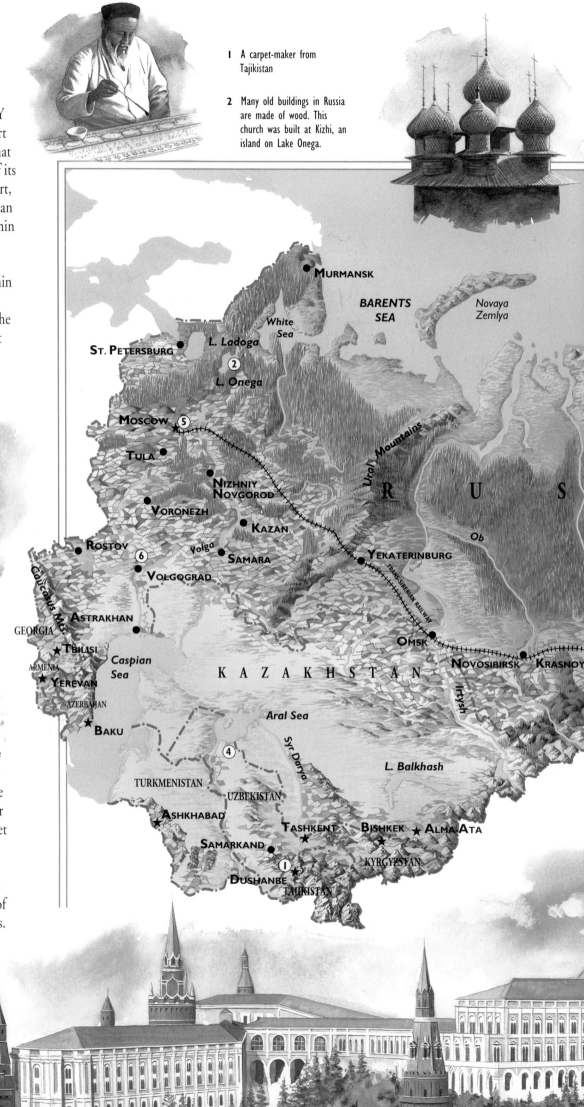

MURMANSK

BARENTS SEA

Novaya Zemlya

White Sea

ST. PETERSBURG

L. Ladoga

2

L. Onega

MOSCOW **5**

TULA

NIZHNIY NOVGOROD

VORONEZH

KAZAN

Volga

SAMARA

Ural Mountains

R U S S

Ob

YEKATERINBURG

ROSTOV

6

VOLGOGRAD

Caucasus Mts.

ASTRAKHAN

GEORGIA

TBILISI

ARMENIA

YEREVAN

AZERBAIJAN

BAKU

Caspian Sea

K A Z A K H S T A N

Aral Sea

Syr Darya

TRANS-SIBERIAN RAILWAY

OMSK

Irtysh

NOVOSIBIRSK

KRASNOY.

L. Balkhash

4

TURKMENISTAN

UZBEKISTAN

ASHKHABAD

SAMARKAND

1

DUSHANBE

TAJIKISTAN

TASHKENT

BISHKEK

ALMA-ATA

KYRGYZSTAN

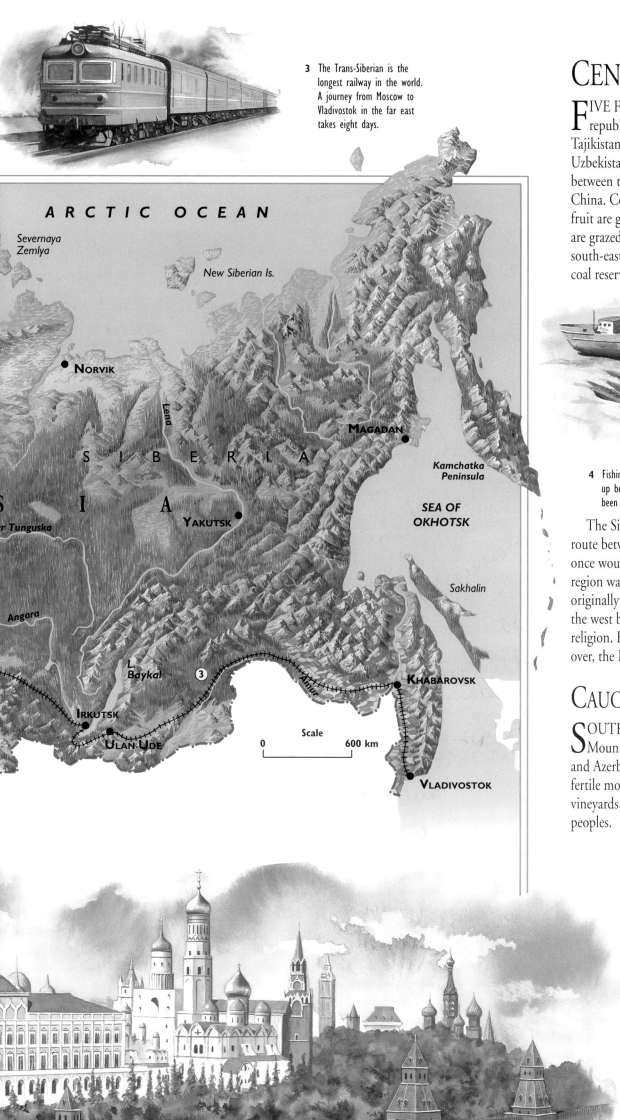

3 The Trans-Siberian is the longest railway in the world. A journey from Moscow to Vladivostok in the far east takes eight days.

35

CENTRAL ASIA

FIVE FORMER SOVIET republics, Kazakhstan, Kyrgyzstan, Tajikistan, Turkmenistan and Uzbekistan, lie in the desert region between the Middle East, Russia and China. Cotton, cereals, tobacco and fruit are grown near the rivers. Sheep are grazed on mountain slopes in the south-east. There are large oil, gas and coal reserves.

4 Fishing boats lie stranded on the dried-up bed of the Aral Sea. Its waters have been used to irrigate cotton.

The Silk Road, the ancient trade route between China and Europe, once wound across Central Asia. The region was settled by Turks (a people originally from the east). Arabs from the west brought with them the Islam religion. Before the Russians took over, the Mongols reigned supreme.

CAUCASUS

SOUTH of the Caucasus Mountains lie Georgia, Armenia and Azerbaijan. This small region of fertile mountain valleys, orchards and vineyards, is home to many different peoples.

5 The Kremlin in Moscow was once a medieval fortress. Within its brick walls are palaces and cathedrals.

THE MIDDLE EAST

THE REGION THAT LIES between the shores of the eastern Mediterranean Sea and the Indian sub-continent is known as the Middle East. Egypt and Afghanistan are often included within the Middle East. In the dry climate, much of the land is scrubland or desert. Farming is only possible on the Mediterranean coast, near the rivers or on irrigated land. The two largest rivers, the Tigris and Euphrates, bring water to Iraq. Thousands of years ago in Mesopotamia, the land lying between these rivers, the ancient empires of Assyria and Babylon grew up.

The Middle East has played an important part in world history in many ways. Three great religions, Judaism, Christianity and Islam, all have their birthplaces here. There are enormous reserves of oil, mined by the countries that border the Persian Gulf. And conflict – between empires, nations and different religious groups – has raged here for centuries.

1 This building has been cut out of a sandstone cliff face at Petra, Jordan. It was once a tomb of a ruler of the Nabataeans, a wandering desert tribe who lived at about the time of Christ. The Romans rebuilt the entrance.

5 A street vendor in Jerusalem (left) pours a glass of tamarindy, a fruit drink.

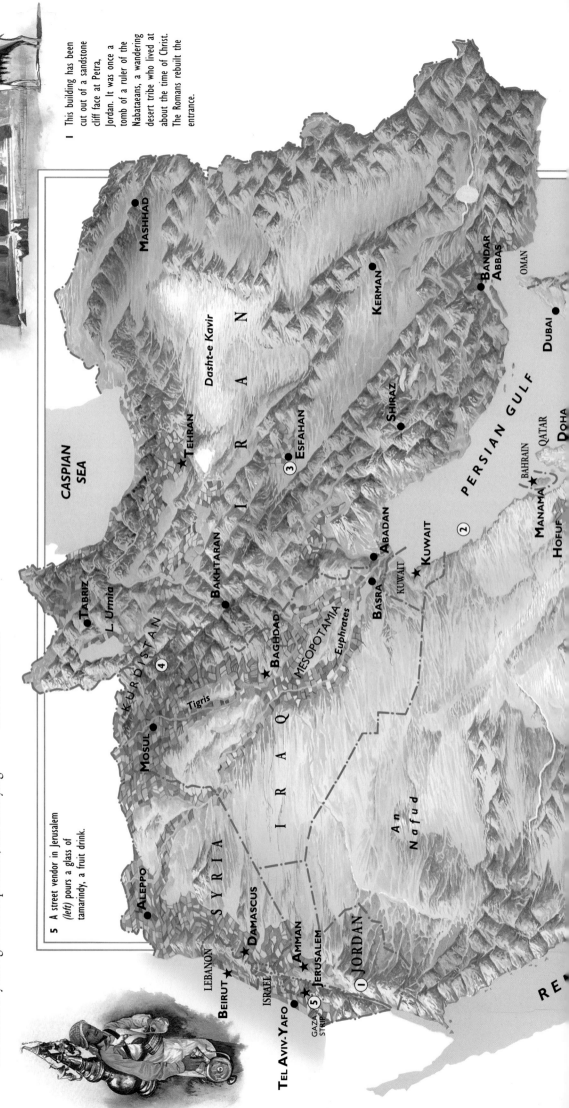

2 Oil is drilled from wells both on land and at sea. This oil rig in the Gulf has a helicopter landing-pad.

EMIRATES

O M A N

S A U D I   A R A B I A

Rub al Khali

ARABIAN SEA

● MECCA

● JIDDAH

★ SAN'A   Y E M E N

● MUKALLA

● ADEN

E A

N

Scale

0 _____ 400 km

3 The royal mosque in the holy Islamic city of Esfahan, Iran

4 This Kurdish woman comes from a mountainous region which crosses the borders of Iran and Iraq.

THE ARABIAN PENINSULA

ALMOST ALL THE LAND which is surrounded on three sides by the Red Sea, the Persian Gulf and the Arabian Sea is desert. Some parts of it, including the completely uninhabited Rub al Khali ('the Empty Quarter'), consist entirely of windblown sand dunes. Apart from oases, only the uplands of the south-west would show as green in a view from space.

Dotted around this wasteland are some of the wealthiest, most modern cities in the world – places like Riyadh, Abu Dhabi and Kuwait. Saudi Arabia and the Gulf States have grown rich from the sale of oil to the rest of the world. In these countries, sea water has been turned into fresh water, enough to supply large populations.

INDIA

R ISING STEEPLY in the north
of India are the great
mountains of the Himalayas
and Karakoram ranges. To the south
lie the plains. Here the Ganges flows
across fertile lowlands covered with
fields of rice, wheat, millet, sugar cane
and grass pasture. In the west, the
plains become desert. Farther south is
the Deccan plateau, a high wedge of
land between the hills called the
Western and Eastern Ghats.

The summer monsoon winds are

6 Farmworkers take a ride on the roof of
a train in India.

very important to most of India. They
bring heavy rains from the Indian
Ocean to the south-west to drench a
land dry for the rest of the year.

The second most populous
country in the world, India has more
than twelve major languages and
several religions. Although many of
India's millions live in the
countryside, there are major cities and
ports, such as Bombay, Madras and
Calcutta. Many people are poor and
depend on farming for a living.

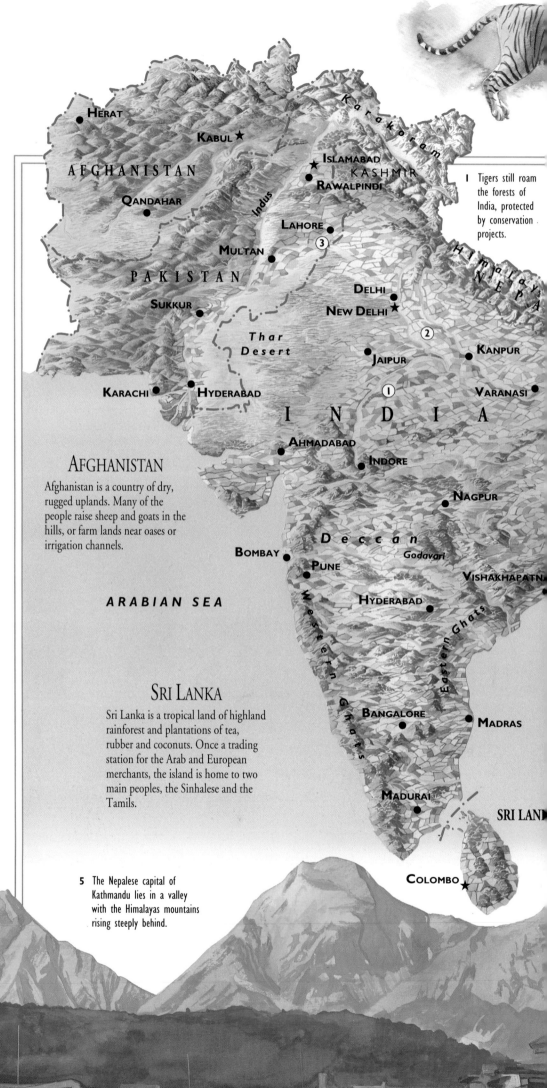

1 Tigers still roam
the forests of
India, protected
by conservation
projects.

AFGHANISTAN

Afghanistan is a country of dry,
rugged uplands. Many of the
people raise sheep and goats in the
hills, or farm lands near oases or
irrigation channels.

ARABIAN SEA

SRI LANKA

Sri Lanka is a tropical land of highland
rainforest and plantations of tea,
rubber and coconuts. Once a trading
station for the Arab and European
merchants, the island is home to two
main peoples, the Sinhalese and the
Tamils.

5 The Nepalese capital of
Kathmandu lies in a valley
with the Himalayas mountains
rising steeply behind.

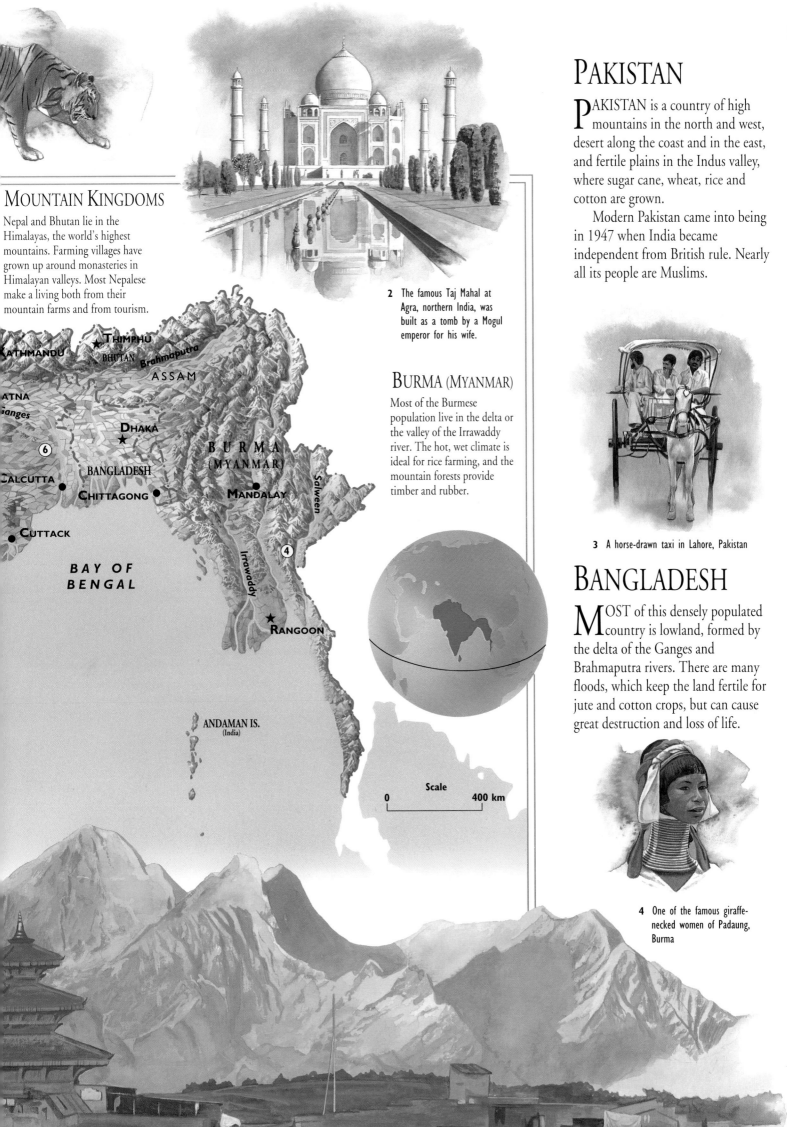

MOUNTAIN KINGDOMS

Nepal and Bhutan lie in the Himalayas, the world's highest mountains. Farming villages have grown up around monasteries in Himalayan valleys. Most Nepalese make a living both from their mountain farms and from tourism.

2 The famous Taj Mahal at Agra, northern India, was built as a tomb by a Mogul emperor for his wife.

BURMA (MYANMAR)

Most of the Burmese population live in the delta or the valley of the Irrawaddy river. The hot, wet climate is ideal for rice farming, and the mountain forests provide timber and rubber.

PAKISTAN

PAKISTAN is a country of high mountains in the north and west, desert along the coast and in the east, and fertile plains in the Indus valley, where sugar cane, wheat, rice and cotton are grown.

Modern Pakistan came into being in 1947 when India became independent from British rule. Nearly all its people are Muslims.

3 A horse-drawn taxi in Lahore, Pakistan

BANGLADESH

MOST of this densely populated country is lowland, formed by the delta of the Ganges and Brahmaputra rivers. There are many floods, which keep the land fertile for jute and cotton crops, but can cause great destruction and loss of life.

4 One of the famous giraffe-necked women of Padaung, Burma

Map labels

THIMPHU
KATHMANDU
BHUTAN
Brahmaputra
ASSAM
PATNA
Ganges
DHAKA
BURMA (MYANMAR)
6
BANGLADESH
CALCUTTA
CHITTAGONG
MANDALAY
Salween
CUTTACK
Irrawaddy
4
BAY OF BENGAL
RANGOON
ANDAMAN IS. (India)

Scale
0   400 km

SOUTH-EAST ASIA

ASIA'S SOUTH-EAST corner is a tropical region. It is hot most of the year with heavy rainfall. South-east Asia consists of the island nations of Indonesia and the Philippines, together with a continental peninsula made up of the countries of Vietnam, Laos, Cambodia and Thailand. Burma or Myanmar (*see page 39*) is sometimes thought of as part of this region.

On the peninsula, there are ricefields in the lowland valleys of the Mekong and Chao Phraya rivers. Forests still cover the highlands of

7 Children cross a bridge over a branch of the Mekong river in southern Vietnam.

northern Thailand, Laos and Vietnam.

Once part of the French empire, Cambodia, Vietnam and Laos have been devastated by wars. Thailand is becoming a modern industrial country. Many tourists visit each year.

Farther south along the Malay peninsula are the rainforests and mountains of Malaysia. This country is one of the world's leading producers of rubber, palm oil and tin. It also includes part of the island of Borneo, which, together with the tiny state of Brunei, has important oil reserves.

More than three-quarters of the population of the island state of Singapore are Chinese. Densely populated, this tiny island is one of the major industrial nations of Asia.

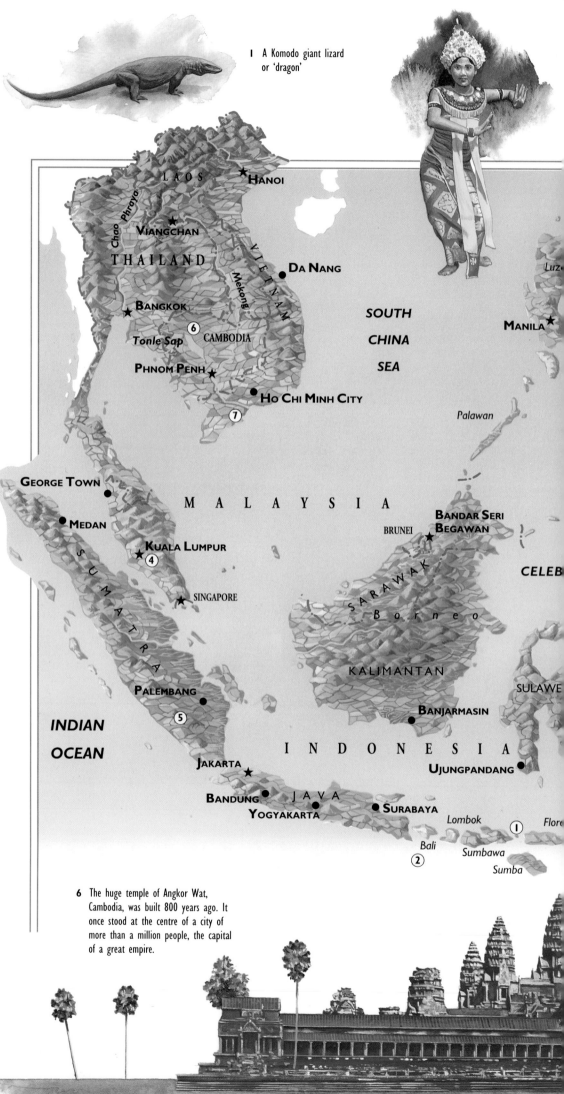

1 A Komodo giant lizard or 'dragon'

6 The huge temple of Angkor Wat, Cambodia, was built 800 years ago. It once stood at the centre of a city of more than a million people, the capital of a great empire.

2 A girl in traditional costume *(left)* dances for visitors to the island of Bali.

3 Off the southern tip of the Philippine island of Mindanao villagers live in houses on stilts *(right)*. Their fishing boats, called *vintas*, have colourful sails.

PACIFIC
OCEAN

PHILIPPINES

THE PHILIPPINES

The Philippines is a country of 7000 islands, rugged mountains and active volcanoes. Once under Spanish, then American rule, nearly all Filipinos are descended from Malay peoples. There are over 70 native languages. Rice is the main crop, grown on both the plains and terraced hillsides of the island of Luzon. Sugar and copra (the source of coconut oil) are cultivated for sale abroad.

CEBU

Mindanao

DAVAO

Moluccas

Ceram

BANDA SEA

WEST IRIAN

PAPUA NEW GUINEA

New Guinea

PORT MORESBY ★

Timor

Scale
0   400 km

INDONESIA

INDONESIA is made up of more than 20,000 islands, the largest island group on Earth. A long chain of volcanoes runs from northern Sumatra to Ceram, of which about 150 are active. One of the greatest eruptions of modern times destroyed the island of Krakatau in 1883.

4 An ox-cart on the streets of Kuala Lumpur, Malaysia

Indonesia lies across the Equator and has a hot, wet climate. Rainforest still covers the highlands and smaller islands; there are more different kinds of plants and animals than in any other of the world's forests. Most of

5 The world's largest flower, *Rafflesia*, is found in Sumatra.

the population lives on the fertile lowlands of Sumatra and Java. Rice, maize and cassava are grown, and there are rubber, sugar cane and coffee plantations.

Indians, Arabs, Chinese and Europeans as well as native peoples live on the islands. Twenty-five different languages are spoken. There are many followers of four great world religions: Islam, Buddhism, Hinduism and Christianity.

CHINA

THE PEOPLE'S REPUBLIC of China is the world's third largest country after Russia and Canada. It has the highest population of any country: well over one billion, or a fifth of all the people in the world.

Very few people live in the mountain and desert regions of the west. They are mainly Mongol, Turkish or Tibetan peoples. The Han, or Chinese-speaking peoples, live in the east. Here, millions of farmers produce rice, maize, wheat, cotton and tea. Huge industrial cities line the great rivers and coastal plains.

To the north, the Huang, or Yellow River, flows across lands of fertile soil, called *loess*, which turns the river the

8 The famous bronze flying horse, just 30 cm high, is about 1800 years old.

colour after which it is named. The fields are planted with cereal crops like wheat and millet. South-eastern China is much wetter and is criss-crossed with canals and wide rivers like the Yangtse. Here, wet-field rice farming is found everywhere.

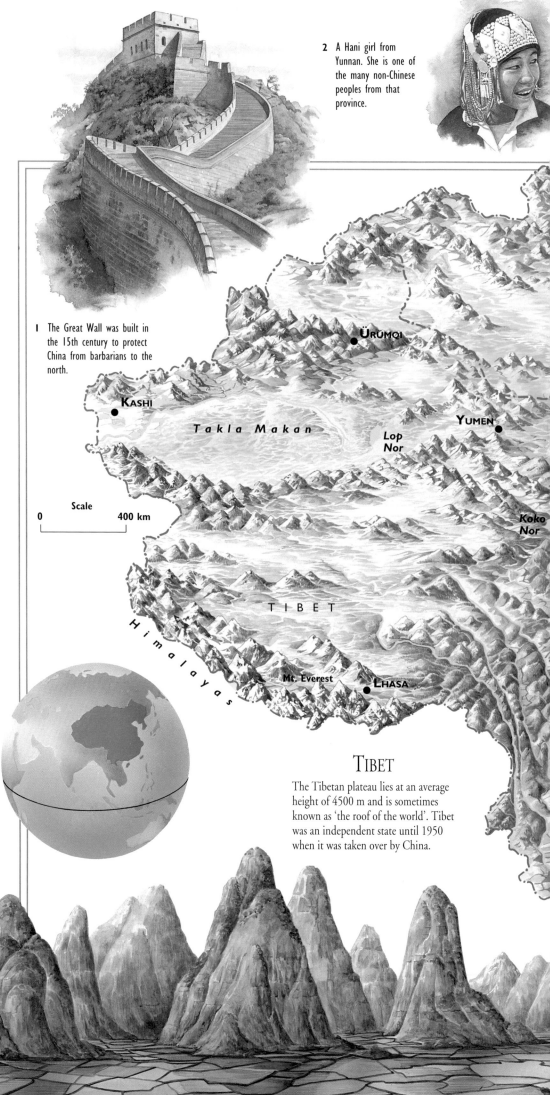

2 A Hani girl from Yunnan. She is one of the many non-Chinese peoples from that province.

1 The Great Wall was built in the 15th century to protect China from barbarians to the north.

ÜRÜMQI

KASHI

Takla Makan

Lop Nor

YUMEN

Koko Nor

T I B E T

H i m a l a y a s

Mt. Everest

LHASA

Scale

0   400 km

TIBET

The Tibetan plateau lies at an average height of 4500 m and is sometimes known as 'the roof of the world'. Tibet was an independent state until 1950 when it was taken over by China.

3 This farmer *(left)* from Sichuan province is off to market to sell his load of fresh poultry.

4 The Temple of Heaven in Beijing *(right)*

MONGOLIA

MONGOLIA was once the centre of the world's greatest-ever empire. Most of the land is mountainous, rocky desert or rough, open grassland, where herdspeople live in their round tents known as *gers*. Mongolia's one large city, Ulan Bator, draws many people away from their traditional way of life.

5 A traditional funeral procession in Korea

KOREA

SINCE THE KOREAN War (1950-53) this ancient kingdom has been split into two. The Communists still rule in the North, while the South has become a fast-growing manufacturing nation, producing electronic goods and cars. The best rice lands are along the southern coast, while most of the minerals – coal, iron, lead, zinc and copper – are found in the North.

6 A Chinese junk sails off Hong Kong harbour

HONG KONG AND MACAO

HONG KONG is a great industrial port. It is due to be returned by Britain to China in 1997. Macao, a tiny peninsula on the other side of the Pearl river will be returned by Portugal in 1999.

TAIWAN

Taiwan has been ruled by the government of the Republic of China since the Communists took over mainland China in 1949. It has grown rich from its electronic and clothing industries.

7 The Xi River near Guilin winds its way through a 'forest' of rounded spires of limestone rock *(left)*.

Map labels

ULAN BATOR

MONGOLIA

HARBIN

SHENYANG

NORTH KOREA

PYONGYANG

SEOUL

SOUTH KOREA

PUSAN

YELLOW SEA

BEIJING

TIANJIN

TAIYUAN

JINAN

QINGDAO

LANZHOU

Huang

Grand Canal

ZHENGZHOU

XI'AN

NANJING

SHANGHAI

CHINA

CHENGDU

WUHAN

Yangtse

EAST CHINA SEA

CHONGQING

CHANGSHA

T'AIPEI

TAIWAN

KUNMING

GUANGZHOU

MACAO (Portugal)

HONG KONG (Br.)

Hainan

JAPAN

JAPAN is made up of four main islands. They are, in order of size, Honshu, Hokkaido, Kyushu and Shikoku. Thickly-forested mountains, many of them volcanic, run the length of the country. The few lowland areas near the coast or along river valleys are shared between great cities like Tokyo, the capital, Osaka and Nagoya, and farmland – mostly rice fields.

With around 5000 earthquakes a year, and the threat of typhoons and huge tidal waves, Japan would seem to be a dangerous place to live! In fact, to the Japanese people, earthquakes are no more than a way of life: most go unnoticed.

Japan is one of the richest industrial countries in the world. It has no natural resources, like oil or minerals, of its own. Japan has become rich from making high-technology goods like cars, CD players and computers.

With so little farmland, the Japanese have turned to the sea as a source of food. More fish is eaten in Japan than anywhere else. Their modern fishing fleet catches more fish than any other country.

1 Hundreds of years ago, just as in Europe, warrior chieftains built large castles to defend themselves and their armies. This is Himeji castle *(above)*, known as the 'White Heron'.

HOKKAIDO

SAPPORO
HAKODATE
AOMORI
SENDAI
NIIGATA

Scale

200 km

0

SEA OF JAPAN

6 The 'Wedded Rocks' stand in the sea off the southern coast. They represent the gods who were supposed to have given birth to the islands of Japan.

7 There are hundreds of natural hot springs in Japan. People bathe in the open air all year round in this spring at Beppu.

5 In Japan, May 5th is called Children's Day. Streamers shaped like fish called carp are flown from the roof tops *(below)*. One carp is flown for every male living in the house

aged seven, five and three put on traditional dress (above) and visit their local shrine or temple. This festival is called *schichi-go-san*, or seven-five-three.

3 Calligraphy, the art of writing, is an admired skill in Japan. Many children are sent to a special school called a *juku*, where they learn to write Japanese characters.

平和日本

4 A high-speed 'bullet train' rushes past Mount Fuji, Japan's most sacred mountain *(below)*. Shaped like a perfect cone, this volcano has not erupted for 300 years.

PACIFIC OCEAN

HONSHU

SHIKOKU

KYUSHU

Tokyo ★
YOKOHAMA
Mt Fuji
NAGOYA
KYOTO
OSAKA
KOBE
WAKAYAMA
OKAYAMA
TAKAMATSU
MATSUYAMA
HIROSHIMA
KITAKYUSHU
FUKUOKA
NAGASAKI
MIYAZAKI

Ryukyu Islands

Okinawa

NATIONS OF OCEANIA

AUSTRALIA
Area 7,682,300 sq km **Population** 17,292,000
Capital Canberra **Language** English

FIJI
Area 18,376 sq km **Population** 746,000
Capital Suva **Languages** Fijian, Hindi, English

KIRIBATI
Area 811 sq km **Population** 72,000
Capital Bairiki **Languages** I-Kiribati, English

NAURU
Area 21 sq km **Pop.** 9000 **Capital** Yaren District
Languages Nauruan, English

3 Australian boy

NEW ZEALAND
Area 270,534 sq km **Population** 3,455,000
Capital Wellington **Languages** English, Maori

PAPUA NEW GUINEA
Area 462,840 sq km **Population** 3,772,000
Capital Port Moresby **Languages** Pidgin,
English, Motu

SOLOMON ISLANDS
Area 27,556 sq km **Population** 319,000
Capital Honiara **Languages** English, Pidgin

1 Boy from Solomon Islands

NORTHERN TERRITORY

Diamonds

Cattle

Emu

Boab tree

Termite mound

Frilled lizard

WESTERN AUSTRALIA

Mining

Manta ray

Kangaroo

Wallaby

Wheat

Road train

Sheep

Sailing

Whale shark

INDIAN OCEAN

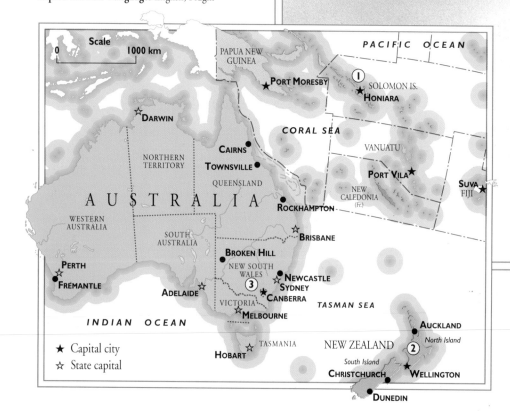

Scale 0 — 1000 km

PAPUA NEW GUINEA

PACIFIC OCEAN

★ PORT MORESBY

① SOLOMON IS.

★ HONIARA

☆ DARWIN

CORAL SEA

CAIRNS ●

VANUATU

TOWNSVILLE ●

PORT VILA ★

NORTHERN TERRITORY

QUEENSLAND

NEW CALEDONIA (Fr.)

SUVA FIJI ★

AUSTRALIA

WESTERN AUSTRALIA

ROCKHAMPTON ●

SOUTH AUSTRALIA

☆ BRISBANE

BROKEN HILL ●

NEW SOUTH WALES

PERTH ☆

③

NEWCASTLE ●

● FREMANTLE

ADELAIDE ☆

SYDNEY ●

★ CANBERRA

VICTORIA

TASMAN SEA

MELBOURNE ●

INDIAN OCEAN

AUCKLAND ●

★ Capital city

TASMANIA

NEW ZEALAND

North Island

②

☆ State capital

HOBART ●

South Island

CHRISTCHURCH ●

★ WELLINGTON

DUNEDIN ●

2 Maori girl from New Zealand

TONGA
Area 748 sq km **Population** 103,000 **Capital**
Nuku'alofa **Languages** Tongan, English

TUVALU
Area 26 sq km **Population** 10,000 **Capital**
Funafuti **Languages** Tuvaluan, English

AUSTRALIA

PAPUA NEW GUINEA

NAURU

KIRIBATI

SOLOMON ISLANDS

VANUATU

TUVALU

FIJI

WESTERN SAMOA

TONGA

NEW ZEALAND

Ore train

ng doctor

Saltwater crocodile

Great Barrier Reef

Snorkelling

Spiny anteater

Mining

QUEENSLAND

Sugar cane

Spinifex grass

Kangaroo

Cattle

Koala

A L I A

L. Eyre

Darling

SOUTH STRALIA

Shepherd

Wheat

Mining

NEW SOUTH WALES

Coal

Grapes

Sheep

Grapes

VICTORIA

Murray

Duck-billed platypus

Gas tanker

TASMANIA

Sperm whale

TASMAN SEA

Cattle

Kiwi

NEW ZEALAND

Sheep

Mt. Cook

Kakapo

Sheep

OCEANIA

OCEANIA is the name given to the group of countries made up of Australia (itself regarded as an island continent), New Zealand, Papua New Guinea and the islands of the Pacific Ocean. *(For a complete map of the Pacific islands see pages 6-7).*

Human beings first arrived in Australia more than 50,000 years ago. Perhaps the first peoples to travel by sea, they came from South-east Asia. A strange new world would have greeted them, for the animal life in Australia was completely different from anywhere else. From there, thousands of years later, people ventured on to the Pacific Islands in their sturdy ocean-going canoes. New Zealand was not reached until around 750 AD.

The first European to set eyes on Australia was a Dutchman, Abel Tasman, who sailed around the coast of Tasmania in 1642. It was not until the late 18th century that Europeans came to live in Australia and New Zealand.

FACTS ABOUT OCEANIA

Area 8,923,000 sq km
Population 26,700,000
Highest point Mt. Cook (New Zealand) 3764 m
Lowest point Lake Eyre (Australia) 16 m below sea level
Longest river Murray-Darling (Australia) 3750 km
Largest lake Lake Eyre (Australia) 9500 sq km
Largest country Australia 7,682,300 sq km
Largest population Australia 17,292,000
Largest city Sydney (Australia) 3,623,500 people

VANUATU
Area 12,190 sq km **Pop.** 157,000 **Capital** Port Vila **Languages** Bislama, English, French
WESTERN SAMOA
Area 2831 sq km **Population** 197,000
Capital Apia **Languages** Samoan, English

AUSTRALIA

AUSTRALIA is about the size of the United States (excluding Alaska). Its population, however, is just seven per cent of the American total. Apart from the south-east and south-west, most of Australia is nearly empty. Inland, much of the land is desert.

Parts of the Northern Territory and Queensland reach into the tropics. The famous Great Barrier Reef fringes

7 The Opera House and Harbour Bridge in Sydney

the eastern coast. Mountains run from the Cape York Peninsula down to Victoria. Most Australians live on the coastal strip to the east. To the west lie farmland and pastures. Some large sheep farms are the size of Wales!

Once, the land belonged to the Aborigines. In the eighteenth century, the first Europeans to settle there were prisoners. Later, as the country's rich minerals were discovered, people from the British Isles, then from all over Europe, came to live in Australia. More recently, immigrants from Asia have made it their home.

1 An Aborigine *(left)* performs a ceremonial dance.

2 The duck-billed platypus *(right)* is one of the Australia's strangest animals. It is a mammal, although it has webbed feet and a beak like a duck's. It even lays eggs!

DARWIN

Cape York Peninsula

NORTHERN TERRITORY

Gibson Desert

QUEENSLA

WESTERN

A U S T R A L

AUSTRALIA

SOUTH

Great Victoria Desert

AUSTRALIA

L. Eyre

GERALDTON

KALGOORLIE

BROKEN HILL

PERTH
FREMANTLE

Great Australian Bight

ADELAIDE

Scale

0   500 km

3 This house *(right)* is built on stilts in the waters of a lagoon off the Solomon Islands. Some villages cluster together on man-made islands built hundreds of years ago.

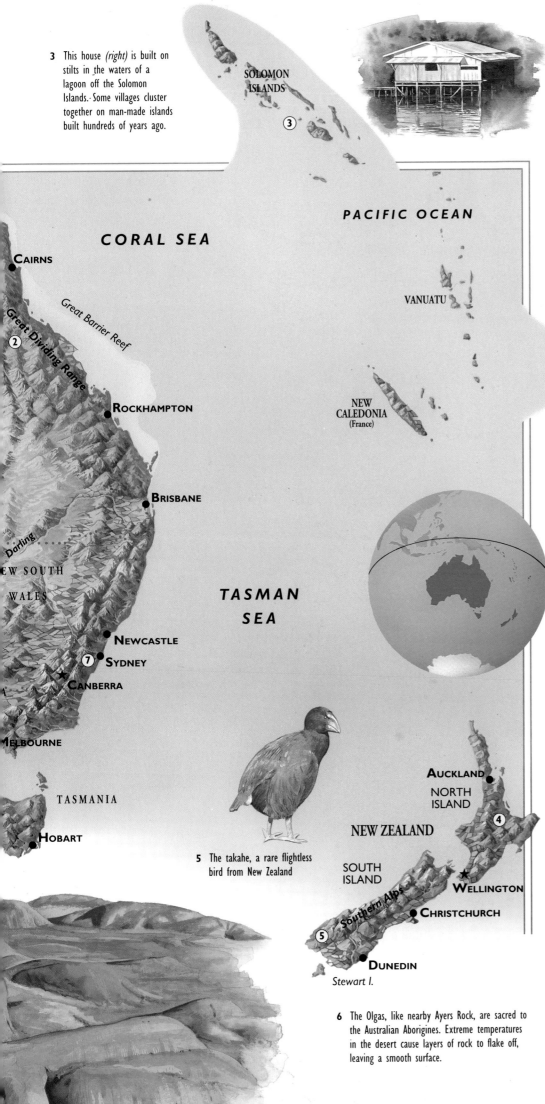

SOLOMON ISLANDS

③

PACIFIC OCEAN

CORAL SEA

CAIRNS

Great Barrier Reef

Great Dividing Range

②

VANUATU

ROCKHAMPTON

NEW CALEDONIA (France)

FIJI

SUVA

BRISBANE

Darling

NEW SOUTH WALES

TASMAN SEA

NEWCASTLE

⑦ SYDNEY

CANBERRA

MELBOURNE

TASMANIA

HOBART

5 The takahe, a rare flightless bird from New Zealand

AUCKLAND

NORTH ISLAND

NEW ZEALAND

④

SOUTH ISLAND

WELLINGTON

Southern Alps

CHRISTCHURCH

⑤

DUNEDIN

Stewart I.

6 The Olgas, like nearby Ayers Rock, are sacred to the Australian Aborigines. Extreme temperatures in the desert cause layers of rock to flake off, leaving a smooth surface.

PACIFIC ISLANDS

DOTTED ACROSS the South Pacific Ocean are thousands of small islands. They are the remains of old volcanoes that once erupted from the ocean floor. Coral reefs in the shape of circles, called atolls, are sometimes all that are left after the volcanoes have vanished beneath the waves. The islanders earn a living from tourism, mining, fishing and exporting fruit and vegetables.

4 Gushing jets of hot water, called geysers, are found in New Zealand.

NEW ZEALAND

NEW ZEALAND is made up of North and South Islands. Both are mountainous, with some volcanoes on North Island. The far north is warm and wet, while the south is cooler. Much of the grassy lowlands are given over to sheep-farming, especially on the plains on South Island. Fruit-growing, vineyards and dairying are also important.

New Zealand was first inhabited by the Maoris, a people who came from other Pacific islands. Europeans, mostly from the British Isles, arrived in the nineteenth century.

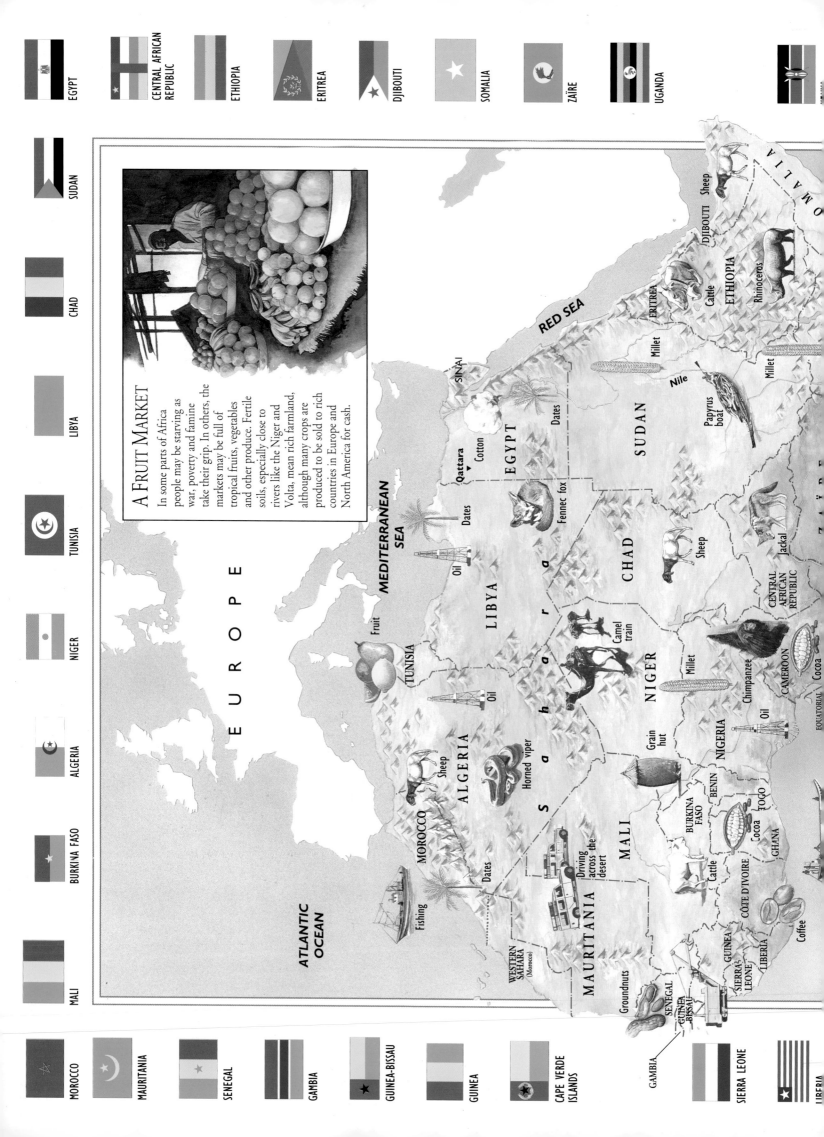

A Fruit Market

In some parts of Africa people may be starving as war, poverty and famine take their grip. In others, the markets may be full of tropical fruits, vegetables and other produce. Fertile soils, especially close to rivers like the Niger and Volta, mean rich farmland, although many crops are produced to be sold to rich countries in Europe and North America for cash.

RWANDA

BURUNDI

TANZANIA

MALAWI

MOZAMBIQUE

SEYCHELLES

COMOROS

MAURITIUS

 SOUTH AFRICA

 MADAGASCAR

 SWAZILAND

 LESOTHO

 ZIMBABWE

 ZAMBIA

 BOTSWANA

 NAMIBIA

 ANGOLA

AFRICA

AFRICA is surrounded by sea except where it meets Asia at the Sinai Peninsula. The second largest continent after Asia, it is three times the size of Europe. The Sahara, the world's largest hot desert, stretches across most of northern Africa. Grasslands and forest cover the low-lying Niger and Congo river basins.

High mountains rise in East Africa on either side of the Great Rift Valley, an enormous gash that slices through the earth's surface from Syria in the Middle East as far as Mozambique. A plateau rises in southern Africa, bordered by mountains in the south-east and desert in the south-west. The savannah grasslands of the plateau are home to thousands of grazing animals.

Man's closest relatives, the chimpanzee and the gorilla, are natives of Africa, and many fossils of early humans suggest that we originally came from this continent, too. Footprints, bones and carved stones show that our ancestors first walked, hunted and learned to use tools in East Africa before setting out to inhabit the rest of the world.

Today, there are hundreds of different peoples living all over Africa, many often sharing the same countries. Both the world's tallest people (the Dinka of Sudan) and the shortest (the Mbuti pygmies of Zaire) live in Africa. Islam is the religion of the north, while both traditional beliefs and Christianity are followed elsewhere.

Europeans have played a big part in African history. In the nineteenth century, Britain, France, Germany, Portugal and others all took part in a 'Scramble for Africa', each taking control of large parts of the continent. Today, all African countries (except Western Sahara) are independent.

FACTS ABOUT AFRICA

Area 29,800,000 sq km
Population 668,700,000
Highest point Kilimanjaro (Tanzania) 5894 m
Lowest point Qattara Depression (Egypt) 132 m below sea level
Longest river Nile 6670 km
Largest lake Victoria 69,500 sq km
Largest country Sudan 2,505,813 sq km
Largest population Nigeria 112,163,000
Largest city Cairo (Egypt) 6,052,800 people

INDIAN OCEAN

Map labels: Dhow, Masai herdsman, COMOROS, MADAGASCAR, Cashew nuts, Chameleon, Zebra, Hippopotamus, MOZAMBIQUE, Tea, TANZANIA, MALAWI, Tobacco, Impala, Gorilla, ZIMBABWE, SWAZILAND, Copper mine, Diamonds, LESOTHO, Leopard, ZAMBIA, BOTSWANA, Elephant, Sheep, Diamonds, Mining, Lion, SOUTH AFRICA, Hornbill, Ostrich, NAMIBIA, ANGOLA

 CÔTE D'IVOIRE

 GHANA

 TOGO

 BENIN

 NIGERIA

CAMEROON

EQUATORIAL GUINEA

SÃO TOMÉ & PRÍNCIPE

 ANGOLA

 NAMIBIA

 BOTSWANA

 CONGO

NATIONS OF AFRICA

ALGERIA
Area 2,381,741 sq km **Population** 25,660,000 **Capital** Algiers **Languages** Arabic, French

ANGOLA
Area 1,246,700 sq km **Population** 10,303,000 **Capital** Luanda **Languages** Portuguese, Bantu languages

BENIN
Area 112,622 sq km **Population** 4,889,000 **Capital** Porto-Novo **Language** French

BOTSWANA
Area 582,000 sq km **Population** 1,348,000 **Capital** Gaborone **Languages** English, Tswana

BURKINA FASO
Area 274,200 sq km **Population** 9,242,000 **Capital** Ouagadougou **Languages** French, Mossi

BURUNDI
Area 27,834 sq km **Population** 5,620,000 **Capital** Bujumbura **Languages** French, Kirundi, Swahili

CAMEROON
Area 475,442 sq km **Population** 12,239,000 **Capital** Yaoundé **Languages** French, English

CAPE VERDE ISLANDS
Area 4033 sq km **Population** 370,000 **Capital** Praia **Languages** Portuguese, Crioulo

CENTRAL AFRICAN REPUBLIC
Area 622,984 sq km **Population** 3,127,000 **Capital** Bangui **Languages** French, Sango

CHAD
Area 1,284,000 sq km **Population** 5,819,000 **Capital** N'Djamena **Languages** French, Arabic

COMOROS
Area 1862 sq km **Population** 335,000 **Capital** Moroni **Languages** Arabic, French

CONGO
Area 342,000 sq km **Population** 2,346,000 **Capital** Brazzaville **Language** French

CÔTE D'IVOIRE
Area 322,462 sq km **Population** 13,765,000 **Capitals** Yamoussoukro, Abidjan **Languages** French, Malinke

DJIBOUTI
Area 23,200 sq km **Population** 520,000 **Capital** Djibouti **Languages** Arabic, French

EGYPT
Area 997,739 sq km **Pop.** 54,688,000 **Capital** Cairo **Language** Arabic

EQUATORIAL GUINEA
Area 28,051 sq km **Pop.** 356,000 **Capital** Malabo **Language** Spanish

ERITREA
Area 121,144 sq km **Pop.** 2,000,000 **Capital** Asmera **Language** Tigrinya

ETHIOPIA
Area 1,128,221 sq km **Population** 49,883,000 **Capital** Addis Ababa **Language** Amharic

GABON
Area 267,667 sq km **Pop.** 1,212,000 **Capital** Libreville **Languages** French, Fang, Bantu languages

GAMBIA
Area 11,295 sq km **Pop.** 884,000 **Capital** Banjul **Language** English

GHANA
Area 238,537 sq km **Population** 16,445,000 **Capital** Accra **Languages** English, Kwa languages

GUINEA
Area 245,857 sq km **Population** 5,931,000 **Capital** Conakry **Languages** French, Soussou, Manika

GUINEA-BISSAU
Area 36,125 sq km **Pop.** 984,000 **Capital** Bissau **Language** Portuguese

KENYA
Area 580,367 sq km **Pop.** 25,905,000 **Capital** Nairobi **Languages** Swahili, Englisi, Kikuyu, Luo

1 Woodabe girl from Niger

6 Berber girl from Morocco

EUROPE

MEDITERRANEAN SEA

RED SEA

Nile
Blue Nile
White Nile

MADEIRA (Port.)
CANARY IS. (Spain)

ORAN
ALGIERS
TUNIS
TUNISIA
TRIPOLI
BANGHAZI
ALEXANDRIA
CAIRO
L. Nasser

RABAT
CASABLANCA
MARRAKECH 6
MOROCCO

WESTERN SAHARA (Morocco)

ALGERIA
LIBYA
EGYPT

NOUAKCHOTT
MAURITANIA

MALI
TOMBOUCTOU
Niger

NIGER
N'DJAMENA
L. Chad
CHAD

BUR SUDAN
KHARTOUM
SUDAN

ASMERA
ERITREA
DJIBOUTI DJIBOUTI
ETHIOPIA
ADDIS ABABA

SOMALIA

DAKAR
SENEGAL
BANJUL
GUINEA-BISSAU
BISSAU
CONAKRY
FREETOWN
SIERRA LEONE
MONROVIA
LIBERIA

BAMAKO
GUINEA

BURKINA FASO
OUAGADOUGOU

NIAMEY
NIGERIA
KANO
ABUJA
LAGOS 5
PORTO-NOVO
BENIN
LOME
TOGO
GHANA
ACCRA
CÔTE D'IVOIRE
YAMOUSSOUKRO
ABIDJAN

CAMEROON
YAOUNDE
MALABO

CENTRAL AFRICAN REPUBLIC
BANGUI

2 Masai girl

3 Efe (pygmy) girl from Zaïre

ATLANTIC OCEAN

INDIAN OCEAN

Scale

0 — 1000 km

★ Capital city

5 Nigerian boy

4 Zulu boy from South Africa

NAMIBIA
Area 824,292 sq km Population 1,837,000 Capital Windhoek
Languages English, Afrikaans, German

NIGER
Area 1,267,000 sq km Population 7,984,000 Capital Niamey Languages French, Hausa, Tuareg, Djerma, Fulani

NIGERIA
Area 923,768 sq km Population 112,163,000 Capital Abuja
Languages English, Hausa, Yoruba, Ibo

RÉUNION
Area 2512 sq km Population 598,000 Capital Saint-Denis Language French

RWANDA
Area 26,338 sq km Population 7,149,000 Capital Kigali Languages French, K.nyarwanda, Swahili

WESTERN SAHARA
Area 266,000 sq km Pop. 200,000
Capital El Aaiun Language Arabic

ZAÏRE
Area 2,344,885 sq km Population 36,672,000 Capital Kinshasa
Languages Swahili, Lingala, French

ZAMBIA
Area 752,614 sq km Population 8,780,000 Capital Lusaka
Languages English, Lozi

ZIMBABWE
Area 39C,759 sq km Population 10,412,000 Capital Harare
Languages English, Shona, Ndebele

SOMALIA
Area 637,657 sq km Pop. 7,691,000
Capital Mogadishu Languages Somali, Arabic, English, Italian

SOUTH AFRICA
Area 1,221,037 sq km Population 36,070,000 Capitals Pretoria, Cape Town
Languages Afrikaans, English, Xhosa, Zulu, Sesotho

SUDAN
Area 2,505,813 sq km Population 25,941,000 Capital Khartoum
Languages Arabic, English

SWAZILAND
Area 17,363 sq km Pop. 817,000 Capital Mbabane Languages English, siSwati

TANZANIA
Area 945,087 sq km Population 28,359,000 Capital Dar es Salaam
Languages Swahili, English

TOGO
Area 56,785 sq km Population 3,643,000 Capital Lomé
Languages French, Kabiye, Ewe

TUNISIA
Area 164,150 sq km Population 8,362,000 Capital Tunis
Languages Arabic, Berber, French

UGANDA
Area 241,139 sq km Pop. 817,000 Capital Kampala
Languages English, Luganda

SÃO TOMÉ AND **PRÍNCIPE**
Area 964 sq km Pop. 124,000 Capital São Tomé Language Portuguese

SENEGAL
Area 196,192 sq km Pop. 7,533,000
Capital Dakar Language French

SEYCHELLES
Area 454 sq km Pop. 68,000 Capital Victoria Languages English, Creole

SIERRA LEONE
Area 71,740 sq km Population 4,260,000 Capital Freetown Languages English, Krio, Mende, Limba, Temne

LESOTHO
Area 30,355 sq km Population 1,826,000 Capital Maseru
Languages English, Sesotho

LIBERIA
Area 97,754 sq km Pop. 2,705,000
Capital Monrovia Language English

LIBYA
Area 1,775,500 sq km Pop. 4,712,000
Capital Tripoli Language Arabic

MADAGASCAR
Area 587,041 sq km Population 11,493,000 Capital Antananarivo
Languages Malagasy, French

MALAWI
Area 118,484 sq km Population 8,556,000 Capital Lilongwe
Languages English, Chichewa

MALI
Area 1,240,192 sq km Pop. 9,507,000
Capital Bamako Language French

MAURITANIA
Area 1,030,700 sq km Pop. 2,036,000
Capital Nouakchott Languages Arabic, Poular, Wolof, Solinke

MAURITIUS
Area 2040 sq km Population 1,059,000
Capital Port Louis Languages English, Creole

MOROCCO
Area 446,550 sq km Population 25,500,000 Capital Rabat Languages Arabic, Berber, Spanish, French

MOZAMBIQUE
Area 799,380 sq km Population 16,084,000 Capital Maputo Languages Portuguese, Ronga, Shangaan, Muchope

NORTHERN AFRICA

REACHING right across Northern Africa is the Sahara, the largest hot desert in the world. About the size of the United States, most of the desert is not sandy at all, but made up of stones, gravel and bare, rocky mountains. Few people live here, but there are oil-wells and even small towns near the oases.

The people of the northern countries are mostly Arabs. Five thousand years ago, the fertile Nile valley in Egypt was the setting for the great civilization of Ancient Egypt. The pyramids and temples are still wondered at today. The Atlas Mountains, home to the Berber people who ruled the region before the Arabs came, separate the

7 This member of the Bamilike people of Cameroon wears a feathered hat and elephant mask for a special ceremony.

farmlands of the north-west from the desert.

South of the Sahara, in West Africa, ancient empires once thrived. People traded gold for salt with the Arabs across the desert. Today there are many nations with industries and sea-ports. Oil-rich Nigeria has the highest population of any country in Africa. Inland from the coast, much of the rainforest is being cut down to

1 The cities of Morocco are well-known for their colourful marketplaces, or *souks*. Fruit, finely embroidered cloths, bags and copperware are among the goods for sale.

ALGIERS
TUNIS
TRI
RABAT
CASABLANCA
MARRAKECH
MADEIRA (Portugal)
MOROCCO
Atlas Mountains
TUNISIA
CANARY IS. (Spain)
A L G E R I A
L
LAS PALMAS
WESTERN SAHARA (Morocco)
S A H A R A
Ahaggar
D
MAURITANIA
M A L I
N I G E R
NOUAKCHOTT
TOMBOUCTOU
Niger
SENEGAL
NIAMEY
L. Chad
DAKAR
GAMBIA
BAMAKO
OUAGADOUGOU
KANO
N'DJAMENA
GUINEA-BISSAU
BURKINA FASO
N I G E R I A
G U I N E A
BENIN
CONAKRY
L. Volta
ABUJA
Benue
SIERRA LEONE
CÔTE D'IVOIRE
GHANA
TOGO
IBADAN
FREETOWN
YAMOUSSOUKRO
LOMÉ
LAGOS
LIBERIA
ACCRA
CAMEROON
MONROVIA
ABIDJAN
DOUALA
YAOUNDÉ
GULF OF GUINEA
EQUATORIAL GUINEA
SÃO TOMÉ AND PRÍNCIPE
Scale
0   400 km

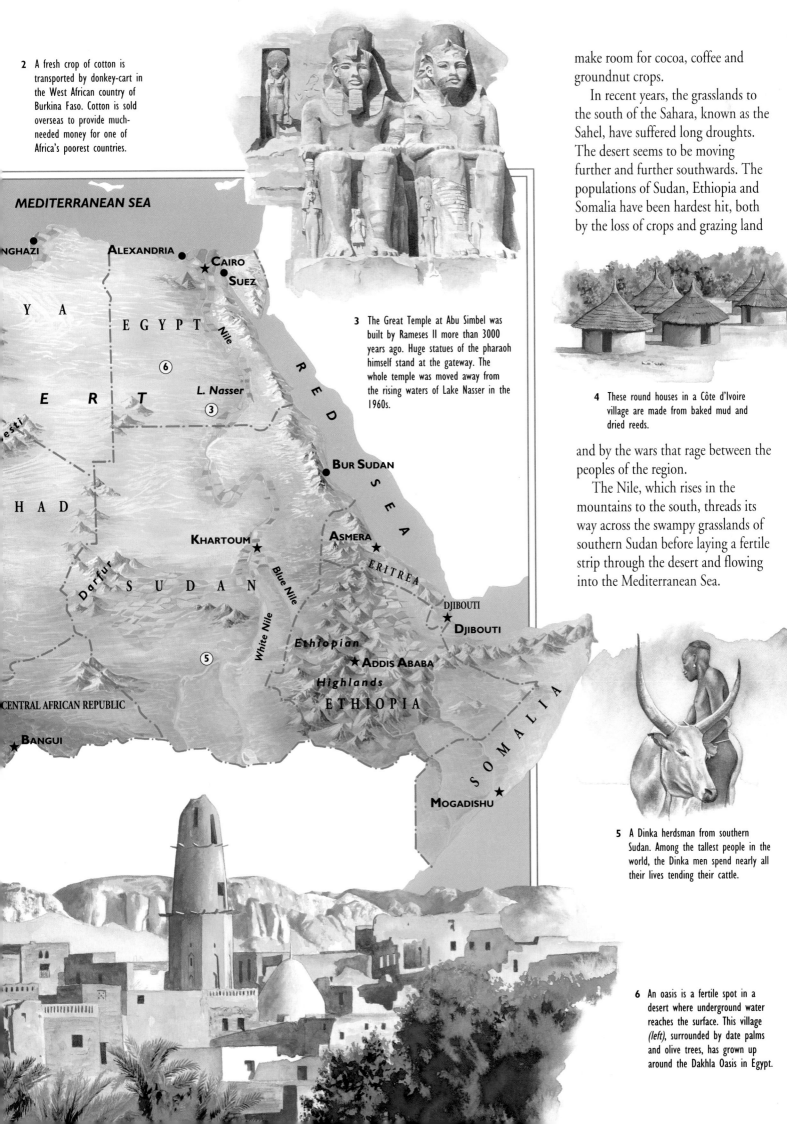

2 A fresh crop of cotton is transported by donkey-cart in the West African country of Burkina Faso. Cotton is sold overseas to provide much-needed money for one of Africa's poorest countries.

MEDITERRANEAN SEA

NGHAZI
ALEXANDRIA
CAIRO
SUEZ

L I B Y A

E G Y P T

⑥

Nile

L. Nasser

③

R E D   S E A

esti

C H A D

BUR SUDAN

KHARTOUM ★

Darfur

S U D A N

Blue Nile

White Nile

ASMERA ★

ERITREA

DJIBOUTI
DJIBOUTI ●

⑤

Ethiopian

★ ADDIS ABABA

Highlands

E T H I O P I A

S O M A L I A

CENTRAL AFRICAN REPUBLIC

★ BANGUI

MOGADISHU ★

3 The Great Temple at Abu Simbel was built by Rameses II more than 3000 years ago. Huge statues of the pharaoh himself stand at the gateway. The whole temple was moved away from the rising waters of Lake Nasser in the 1960s.

make room for cocoa, coffee and groundnut crops.

In recent years, the grasslands to the south of the Sahara, known as the Sahel, have suffered long droughts. The desert seems to be moving further and further southwards. The populations of Sudan, Ethiopia and Somalia have been hardest hit, both by the loss of crops and grazing land

4 These round houses in a Côte d'Ivoire village are made from baked mud and dried reeds.

and by the wars that rage between the peoples of the region.

The Nile, which rises in the mountains to the south, threads its way across the swampy grasslands of southern Sudan before laying a fertile strip through the desert and flowing into the Mediterranean Sea.

5 A Dinka herdsman from southern Sudan. Among the tallest people in the world, the Dinka men spend nearly all their lives tending their cattle.

6 An oasis is a fertile spot in a desert where underground water reaches the surface. This village (left), surrounded by date palms and olive trees, has grown up around the Dakhla Oasis in Egypt.

SOUTHERN AFRICA

MUCH OF THE SOUTHERN HALF of Africa is high ground, but quite flat, like a table. This plateau is rimmed by mountains in the far south, the Drakensberg, and in the east, where ranges follow the line of the Great Rift Valley. Great rivers flow off the plateau to the north. Here, near the Equator, they wind through the Congo basin rainforest. On higher land, the forests give way to savanna – dry grasslands dotted with trees. Enormous numbers of animals gather on the savanna to feed on the grasses. In the southwest, the climate is drier and the savanna turns to desert.

The Bantu people, herdsmen and farmers from West Africa have made Southern Africa their home. Many years ago, they took over the land from the Bushmen or Khoisan peoples, who lived by hunting. Europeans and Asians have also settled here, working the fertile farmlands and building trading ports. Mining for diamonds, copper, gold and other minerals is an important industry today.

1 The savanna grasslands are famous for the great herds of animals that graze there. Many parks and game reserves now protect the giraffes (above), zebras, lions, elephants, wildebeest and other animals.

2 This woman is from Mozambique, a country that was once governed by Portugal. She rubs a cream made from ground bark into her skin to keep it moist in the hot sun.

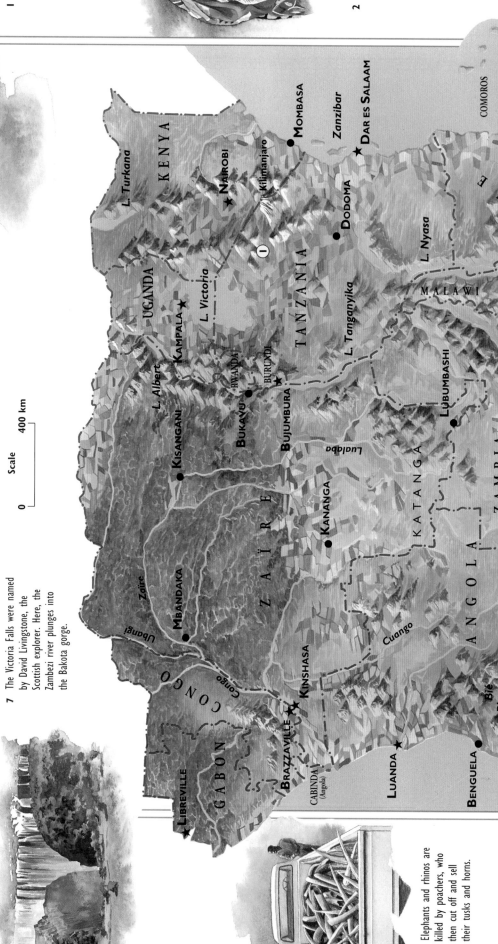

Scale

0   400 km

COMOROS

MOMBASA

Zanzibar

DAR ES SALAAM

KENYA

L. Turkana

NAIROBI

Kilimanjaro

DODOMA

L. Nyasa

UGANDA

L. Victoria

TANZANIA

L. Tanganyika

MALAWI

KAMPALA

L. Albert

RWANDA

BUKAVU

BURUNDI

BUJUMBURA

Lualaba

KISANGANI

KATANGA

LUBUMBASHI

Z A Ï R E

KANANGA

ZAMBIA

MBANDAKA

Zaïre

Ubangi

Cuango

ANGOLA

Congo

CONGO

KINSHASA

BRAZZAVILLE

CABINDA (Angola)

Bie Plateau

GABON

LIBREVILLE

LUANDA

BENGUELA

7 The Victoria Falls were named by David Livingstone, the Scottish explorer. Here, the Zambezi river plunges into the Bakota gorge.

6 Elephants and rhinos are killed by poachers, who then cut off and sell their tusks and horns.

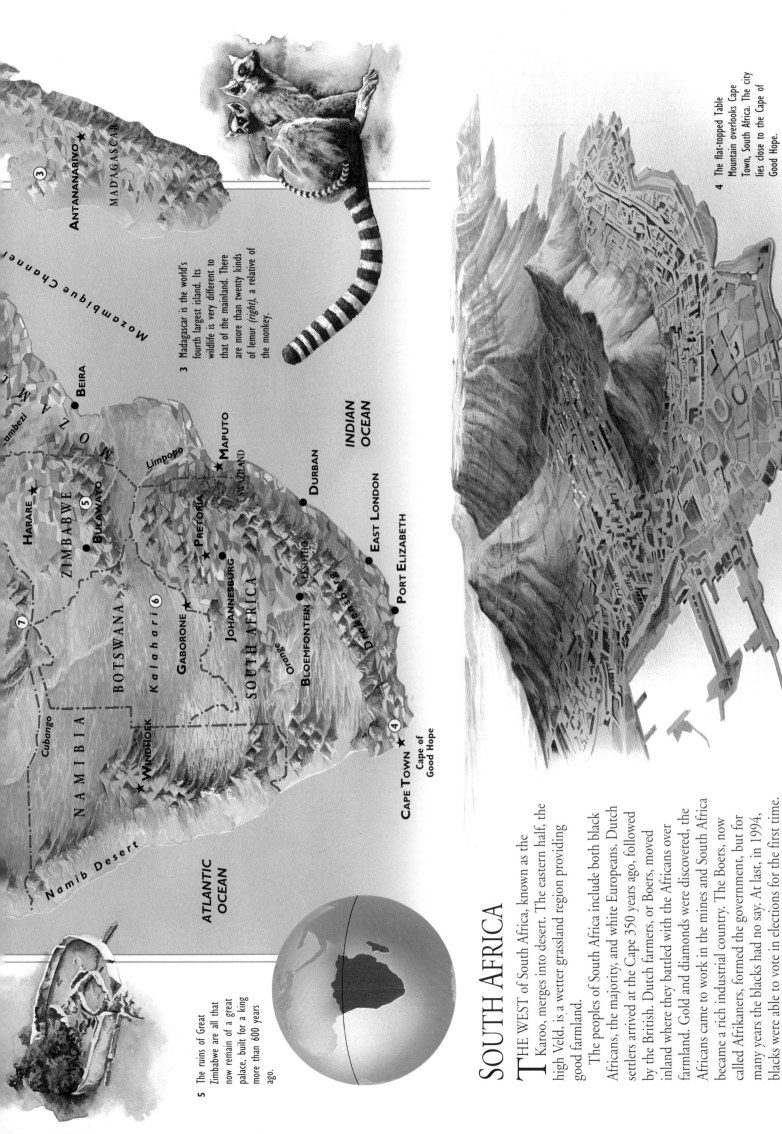

57

③

ANTANANARIVO

MADAGASCAR

Mozambique Channel

3 Madagascar is the world's fourth largest island. Its wildlife is very different to that of the mainland. There are more than twenty kinds of lemur *(right)*, a relative of the monkey.

BEIRA

Zambezi

Limpopo

MAPUTO

SWAZILAND

DURBAN

EAST LONDON

PORT ELIZABETH

INDIAN OCEAN

HARARE

ZIMBABWE ⑤

BULAWAYO

PRETORIA

JOHANNESBURG

LESOTHO

Drakensberg

BLOEMFONTEIN

Orange

SOUTH AFRICA

NAMIBIA

BOTSWANA

Kalahari ⑥

GABORONE

WINDHOEK

⑦

Cubango

Namib Desert

ATLANTIC OCEAN

CAPE TOWN
Cape of
Good Hope

④

4 The flat-topped Table Mountain overlooks Cape Town, South Africa. The city lies close to the Cape of Good Hope.

5 The ruins of Great Zimbabwe are all that now remain of a great palace, built for a king more than 600 years ago.

SOUTH AFRICA

THE WEST of South Africa, known as the Karoo, merges into desert. The eastern half, the high Veld, is a wetter grassland region providing good farmland.

The peoples of South Africa include both black Africans, the majority, and white Europeans. Dutch settlers arrived at the Cape 350 years ago, followed by the British. Dutch farmers, or Boers, moved inland where they battled with the Africans over farmland. Gold and diamonds were discovered, the Africans came to work in the mines and South Africa became a rich industrial country. The Boers, now called Afrikaners, formed the government, but for many years the blacks had no say. At last, in 1994, blacks were able to vote in elections for the first time.

HAITI

DOMINICAN REPUBLIC

ST. KITTS AND NEVIS

ANTIGUA & BARBUDA

GREENLAND

CUBA

JAMAICA

BAHAMAS

CANADA

UNITED STATES OF AMERICA

MEXICO

GUATEMALA

BELIZE

HONDURAS

EL SALVADOR

ARCTIC OCEAN

GREENLAND
(Denmark)

CANADA

ALASKA
(US)

UNITED STATES

Narwhal

Fishing

Grey seal

Container ship

Potatoes

Mining

New York taxi

Storing grain

Baffin I.

Beaver

Moose

Mining

Walrus

Polar bear

Industry

L. Superior

Hudson Bay

Beluga whale

Timber

Cattle

Arctic tern

Wheat

Arctic fox

Snowmobile

Mining

Maize

Prairie dog

Coyote

Missouri

Harvesting wheat

Caribou

Polar bear

Brown bear

Rocky Mountains

Timber

Aircraft factory

Potatoes

Bingham Canyon mine

Death Valley ▼

Grey whale

Oil

Musk ox

Oil pipeline

Mining

Mt. McKinley ▲

Bering Strait

Lynx

Oil tanker

Salmon

Grapes

Oranges

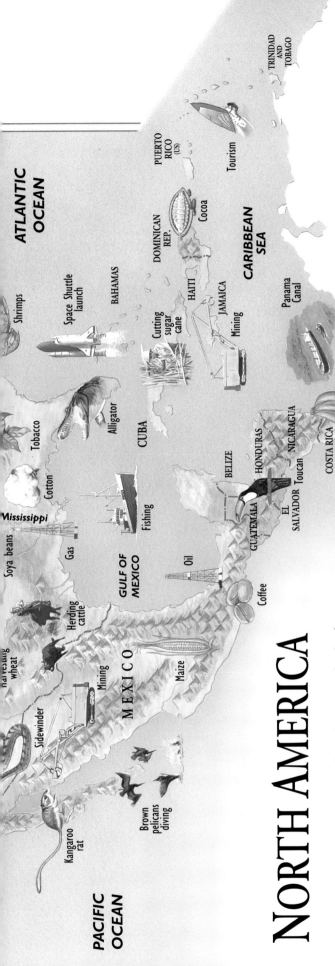

NORTH AMERICA

NORTH AMERICA stretches from the Arctic islands of Greenland and northern Canada with their permanent ice caps, to the hot, tropical rainforests of the Caribbean coast. From Alaska to Panama, a chain of mountains runs like a backbone down the western side of the continent. In the United States and Mexico it divides into several ranges separated by desert plateaux. Apart from the Appalachians in eastern United States, much of the rest of the land is low-lying.

Humans first settled in North America during the Ice Ages, perhaps around 12,000 years ago. The Bering Strait, which separates North America from Asia, was then dry land and people could simply walk across. The first Americans spread out across the continent and lived by hunting the animals they found there. In Mexico and Central America they became farmers and later founded great civilizations.

Europeans first set eyes on North America about 1000 years ago, when Norse settlers arrived off the east coast of Canada. Only after Christopher Columbus' voyage of discovery in 1492 did Spanish, English and French explorers begin to travel inland across the New World, to be followed by immigrants from Europe and, later, from European colonies in Africa.

FACTS ABOUT NORTH AMERICA

Area 24,250,000 sq km
Population 438,200,000
Highest point Mt. McKinley (Alaska, USA) 6194 m
Lowest point Death Valley (California, USA) 86 m below sea level
Longest river Mississippi-Missouri (USA) 5970 km
Largest lake Superior (Canada and USA) 82,100 sq km
Largest country Canada 9,958,319 sq km
Largest population United States of America 256,420,000
Largest city Mexico City (Mexico) 15,000,000 people

PACIFIC OCEAN

ATLANTIC OCEAN

SOUTH AMERICA

CARIBBEAN SEA

GULF OF MEXICO

Mississippi

MEXICO

CUBA

BAHAMAS

HAITI

DOMINICAN REP.

PUERTO RICO (US)

JAMAICA

BELIZE

GUATEMALA

HONDURAS

EL SALVADOR

NICARAGUA

COSTA RICA

PANAMA

TRINIDAD AND TOBAGO

Kangaroo rat

Brown pelicans diving

Sidewinder

Mining

Maize

Oil

Harvesting wheat

Herding cattle

Gas

Soya beans

Cotton

Tobacco

Shrimps

Space Shuttle launch

Alligator

Cutting sugar cane

Cocoa

Mining

Fishing

Coffee

Toucan

Bananas

Panama Canal

Tourism

NICARAGUA

COSTA RICA

PANAMA

TRINIDAD & TOBAGO

GRENADA

ST. VINCENT AND THE GRENADINES

BARBADOS

ST. LUCIA

DOMINICA

NATIONS OF NORTH AMERICA

60

ANGUILLA
Area 91 sq km **Population** 8960
Capital The Valley **Language** English

ANTIGUA AND BARBUDA
Area 442 sq km **Population** 66,000
Capital St. John's **Language** English

BAHAMAS
Area 13,939 sq km **Population** 258,000
Capital Nassau **Language** English

BARBADOS
Area 430 sq km **Population** 255,000
Capital Bridgetown **Language** English

BELIZE
Area 22,965 sq km **Population** 170,000
Capital Belmopan **Languages** English, Spanish

BERMUDA
Area 53 sq km **Population** 59,000
Capital Hamilton **Language** English

BRITISH VIRGIN ISLANDS
Area 153 sq km **Population** 17,000
Capital Road Town **Language** English

CANADA
Area 9,958,319 sq km **Population** 27,409,000
Capital Ottawa **Languages** English, French

COSTA RICA
Area 50,700 sq km **Population** 3,064,000
Capital San José **Language** Spanish

CUBA
Area 110,860 sq km **Population** 10,736,000
Capital Havana **Language** Spanish

DOMINICA
Area 750 sq km **Pop.** 72,000 **Capital**
Roseau **Languages** English, Creole

DOMINICAN REPUBLIC
Area 48,422 sq km
Population 7,321,000 **Capital** Santo
Domingo **Language** Spanish

EL SALVADOR
Area 21,041 sq km **Population**
5,376,000 **Capital** San Salvador
Language Spanish

GREENLAND
Area 2,175,600 sq km **Population**
57,000 **Capital** Godthåb
Languages Inuit, Danish

GRENADA
Area 345 sq km **Population** 98,000
Capital St. George's
Languages English, French patois

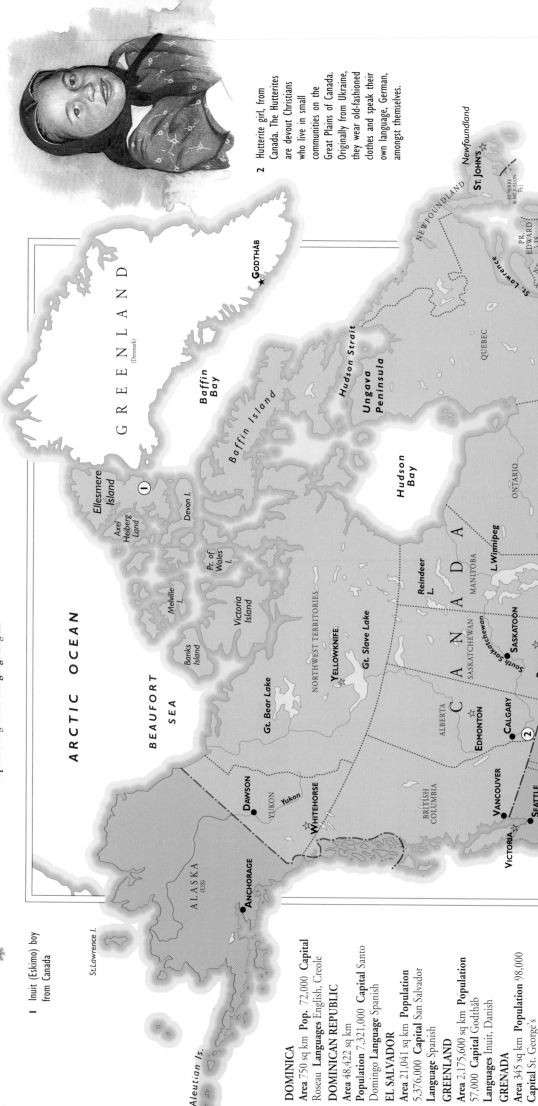

1 Inuit (Eskimo) boy
from Canada

2 Hutterite girl, from
Canada. The Hutterites
are devout Christians
who live in small
communities on the
Great Plains of Canada.
Originally from Ukraine,
they wear old-fashioned
clothes and speak their
own language, German,
amongst themselves.

3 American boy

A VIRGIN IS. (Br. & US)
B ST. MARTIN (Fr. & Neths.)
C ANGUILLA (Br.)
D ST. KITTS AND NEVIS
E ANTIGUA AND BARBUDA
F GUADELOUPE (Fr.)
G DOMINICA

H MARTINIQUE (Fr.)
I ST. LUCIA
J ST. VINCENT AND THE GRENADINES
K BARBADOS
L GRENADA

4 Boy from Caribbean Islands

Map labels

ATLANTIC OCEAN

NEW YORK
PHILADELPHIA
WASHINGTON, D.C.
BALTIMORE
CLEVELAND
CINCINNATI
DETROIT
CHICAGO
MILWAUKEE
L. Ontario
L. Erie
L. Michigan
Ohio

BAHAMAS
NASSAU

ATLANTA

MIAMI

CUBA
HAVANA

Gulf of Mexico

JAMAICA
KINGSTON

CARIBBEAN SEA

HAITI
PORT-AU-PRINCE
DOMINICAN REPUBLIC
SANTO DOMINGO
SAN JUAN
PUERTO RICO (U.S.)
NETHS. ANTILLES

TRINIDAD AND TOBAGO
PORT OF SPAIN

NEW ORLEANS
Mississippi
Arkansas

ST. LOUIS
KANSAS CITY
DALLAS
HOUSTON

UNITED STATES

DENVER
Colorado
SALT LAKE CITY
Snake
PHOENIX
LOS ANGELES
SAN DIEGO
SAN FRANCISCO
MEXICALI

Rio Grande

MEXICO
MONTERREY
GUADALAJARA
MEXICO CITY
MÉRIDA
VILLAHERMOSA

Gulf of California

PACIFIC OCEAN

BELIZE
BELMOPAN
GUATEMALA
SAN SALVADOR
EL SALVADOR
HONDURAS
TEGUCIGALPA
NICARAGUA
MANAGUA
COSTA RICA
SAN JOSÉ
PANAMA

Scale

Scale
0   800 km

★ Capital city
☆ Provincial capital

See pages 66-67 for state names and capitals in the United States of America

Country fact boxes

MEXICO
Area 1,972,547 sq km Population 87,836,000 Capital Mexico City Language Spanish

MONTSERRAT
Area 102 sq km Population 11,000 Capital Plymouth Language English

NETHERLANDS ANTILLES
Area 800 sq km Population 189,000 Capital Willemstad Languages Dutch, Papiamento

NICARAGUA
Area 130,000 sq km Population 3,999,000 Capital Managua Languages Spanish, English

PANAMA
Area 75,517 sq km Population Capital Panama Language Spanish

PUERTO RICO
Area 8959 sq km Population 3,522,000 Capital San Juan Languages Spanish, English

ST. KITTS AND NEVIS
Area 262 sq km Population 44,000 Capital Basseterre Language English

ST. LUCIA
Area 616 sq km Population 153,000 Capital Castries Languages English, French patois

ST. VINCENT AND THE GRENADINES
Area 388 sq km Population 117,000 Capital Kingstown Language English

TRINIDAD AND TOBAGO
Area 5127 sq km Population 1,253,000 Capital Port of Spain Languages English, French, Spanish, Hindi, Chinese

UNITED STATES OF AMERICA
Area 9,372,614 sq km Population 256,420,000 Capital Washington, D.C. Languages English. Spanish

US VIRGIN ISLANDS
Area 355 sq km Population 102,000 Capital Charlotte Amalie Languages English, Spanish, Creole

6 Hopi girl from the United States

GUADELOUPE
Area 1779 sq km Population 387,000 Capital Basse-Terre Languages French, Creole

GUATEMALA
Area 108,889 sq km Population 9,745,000 Capital Guatemala Language Spanish

HAITI
Area 27,750 sq km Population 6,625,000 Capital Port-au-Prince Languages French, Creole

HONDURAS
Area 112,088 sq km Population 4,916,000 Capital Tegucigalpa Language Spanish

JAMAICA
Area 10,991 sq km Pop. 2,461,000 Capital Kingston Language English

MARTINIQUE
Area 1102 sq km Population 360,000 Capital Fort-de-France Languages French, Creole

5 Guatemalan girl

CANADA

THE SECOND LARGEST country in the world, Canada is a land of rugged mountains, many lakes, vast forests and icy wastes. Cities and farmland are found only in the south of the country, near the border with the United States.

Western Canada is dominated by the Rocky and Coast mountain ranges. There are high peaks and deep valleys. The far north of Canada, including the islands bordering the Arctic Ocean, is a frozen desert. The

1 Grain harvested from the fields is stored in these grain elevators before being taken by rail to cities and ports.

6 Part of a totem pole carved by Native Americans from British Columbia

landscape, barren and treeless, is called the tundra. Just beneath the surface, the ground is permanently frozen. Only in the summer, when the top layer of soil melts, do small plants grow, and the caribou and musk ox arrive to feed on them.

The tundra stretches from the far north-west across to Labrador in the east. Farther south, it gives way to flat, thickly forested country pitted with

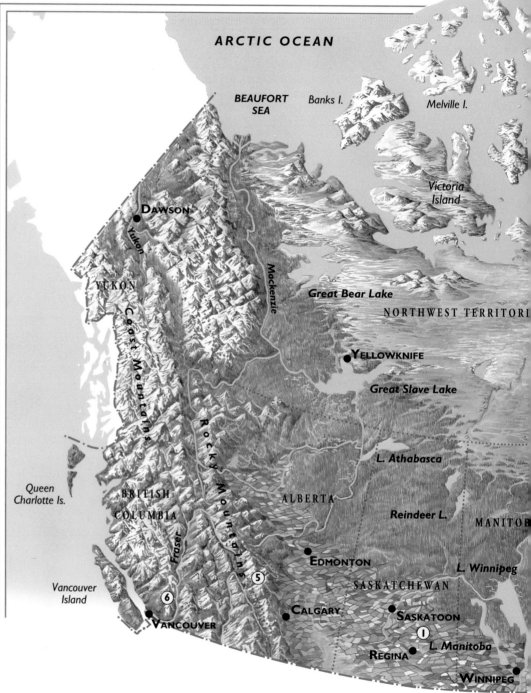

ARCTIC OCEAN

BEAUFORT SEA

Banks I.

Melville I.

Victoria Island

DAWSON

Yukon

YUKON

Coast Mountains

Mackenzie

Great Bear Lake

NORTHWEST TERRITORI

YELLOWKNIFE

Great Slave Lake

L. Athabasca

Rocky Mountains

Queen Charlotte Is.

BRITISH COLUMBIA

Fraser

ALBERTA

Reindeer L.

MANITOB

EDMONTON

L. Winnipeg

5

SASKATCHEWAN

6

Vancouver Island

CALGARY

SASKATOON

1

L. Manitoba

VANCOUVER

REGINA

WINNIPEG

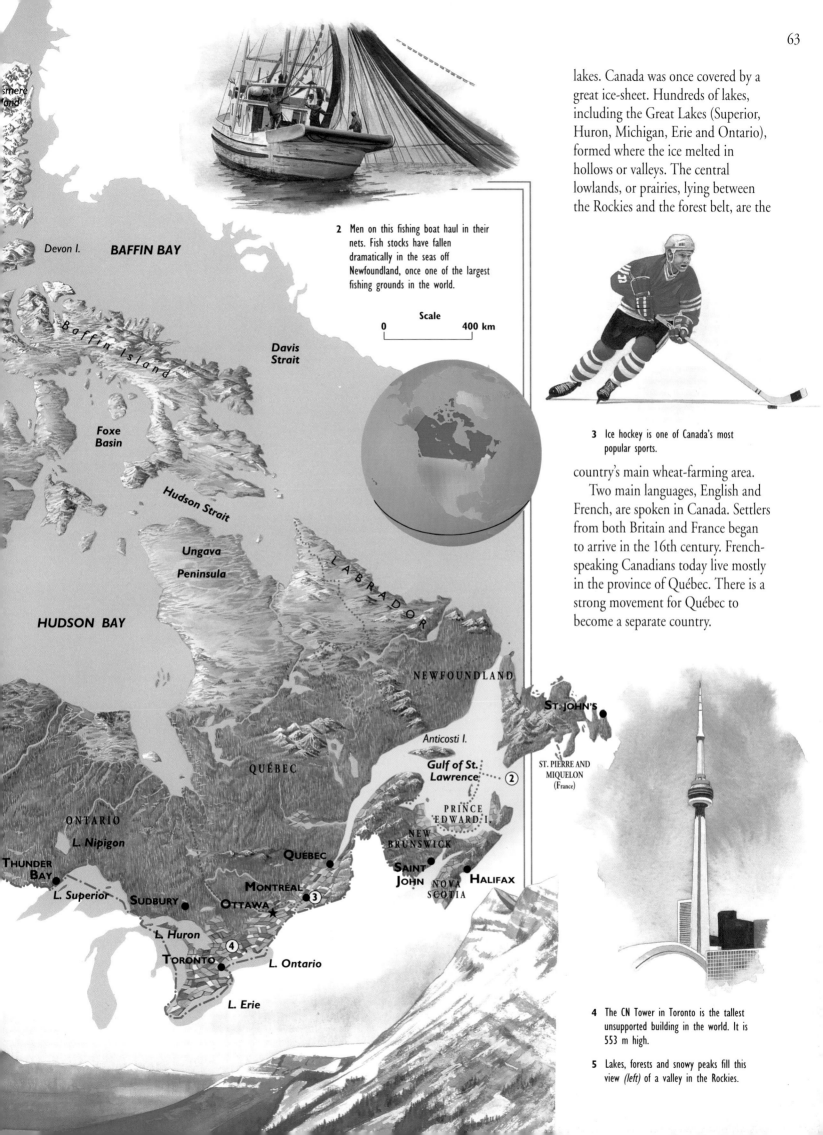

lakes. Canada was once covered by a great ice-sheet. Hundreds of lakes, including the Great Lakes (Superior, Huron, Michigan, Erie and Ontario), formed where the ice melted in hollows or valleys. The central lowlands, or prairies, lying between the Rockies and the forest belt, are the country's main wheat-farming area.

Two main languages, English and French, are spoken in Canada. Settlers from both Britain and France began to arrive in the 16th century. French-speaking Canadians today live mostly in the province of Québec. There is a strong movement for Québec to become a separate country.

2 Men on this fishing boat haul in their nets. Fish stocks have fallen dramatically in the seas off Newfoundland, once one of the largest fishing grounds in the world.

Scale

0   400 km

3 Ice hockey is one of Canada's most popular sports.

4 The CN Tower in Toronto is the tallest unsupported building in the world. It is 553 m high.

5 Lakes, forests and snowy peaks fill this view *(left)* of a valley in the Rockies.

Devon I.   **BAFFIN BAY**

Baffin Island

Foxe Basin

Davis Strait

Hudson Strait

Ungava Peninsula

LABRADOR

HUDSON BAY

NEWFOUNDLAND

St. John's

Anticosti I.

Gulf of St. Lawrence

ST. PIERRE AND MIQUELON (France)

QUÉBEC

PRINCE EDWARD I.

NEW BRUNSWICK

ONTARIO

L. Nipigon

Québec

SAINT JOHN

HALIFAX

NOVA SCOTIA

THUNDER BAY

L. Superior

SUDBURY

MONTRÉAL

OTTAWA

L. Huron

TORONTO

L. Ontario

L. Erie

UNITED STATES

THE FOURTH LARGEST country in the world, the United States of America stretches from the Atlantic to Pacific Oceans. It comprises 50 states, including the Pacific islands of Hawaii, and Alaska, the largest state, which borders northwestern Canada.

The first European settlements were made in the north-east, a region now studded with large industrial cities. The forested Appalachian Mountains divide the coastal plain from the great basin of the river Mississippi – a vast patchwork of

6 The trunk of this giant sequoia tree in California is so massive a car can drive through it.

farmland. Crops include wheat, maize, soya beans and sugar beet in northern and central parts, cotton, tobacco and groundnuts in the south.

West of the Mississippi, the land gradually rises. The grasslands of the

5 In this landscape *(below)*, softer rocks have been worn away to leave the mesas (flat-topped hills) and buttes (rock pillars) of Monument Valley, Arizona.

1 The Golden Gate Bridge *(left)* crosses the entrance to San Francisco Bay. Sometimes fog from the Pacific rolls in beneath it.

2 The Gateway Arch *(right)*, in St. Louis, Missouri, is the tallest monument in the world.

L. Superior

L. Huron

MINNESOTA

WISCONSIN

MICHIGAN

L. Michigan

INNEAPOLIS

MILWAUKEE

DETROIT

L. Erie

L. Ontario

BUFFALO

NEW YORK

MAINE

VT.

N.H.

MASS.

CONN.   R.I.

BOSTON

IOWA

CHICAGO

CLEVELAND

PENNSYLVANIA

N.J.

NEW YORK

MAHA

ILLINOIS

INDIANAPOLIS

OHIO

CINCINNATI

PITTSBURGH

PHILADELPHIA

BALTIMORE

MD.

DEL.

WASHINGTON, D.C.

3

Mississippi

ST LOUIS

2

INDIANA

Ohio

WEST VIRGINIA

VIRGINIA

ANSAS CITY

MISSOURI

KENTUCKY

Appalachian Mountains

NORTH CAROLINA

ATLANTIC OCEAN

Arkansas

TENNESSEE

ARKANSAS

MEMPHIS

Mississippi

MISSISSIPPI

BIRMINGHAM

ATLANTA

SOUTH CAROLINA

ALABAMA

GEORGIA

JACKSONVILLE

LOUISIANA

4

HOUSTON

NEW ORLEANS

FLORIDA

TAMPA

MIAMI

GULF OF MEXICO

Great Plains eventually meet the high Rocky Mountains. Farther west, the climate becomes much drier, and the land is mostly desert or scrub.

The Pacific coast is a land of forested mountains and fertile valleys with a warm, wet climate. Since the first European settlers arrived there in the 19th century, this region has grown to become one of the richest

3 The United States Capitol in Washington, D.C.

and most densely populated parts of the United States.

The Native Americans had America to themselves for 10,000 years. Settlers from Europe spread out across the country only about 200 years ago. Some southern states and

4 A jazz club in New Orleans, Louisiana

northern cities have large black populations, descendants of Africans brought over to work on the cotton plantations. More recently, Latin Americans have come to live in some states, notably California, Texas and Florida.

STATES OF THE USA

ALABAMA
Area 135,775 sq km **Population** 4,128,000
Capital Montgomery **Largest city** Birmingham

ALASKA
Area 1,700,139 sq km **Population** 564,000
Capital Juneau **Largest city** Anchorage

ARIZONA
Area 295,267 sq km **Population** 3,872,000
Capital and largest city Phoenix

ARKANSAS
Area 137,742 sq km **Population** 2,410,000
Capital and largest city Little Rock

CALIFORNIA
Area 424,002 sq km **Population** 31,310,000
Capital Sacramento **Largest city** Los Angeles

COLORADO
Area 269,620 sq km **Population** 3,410,000
Capital and largest city Denver

CONNECTICUT
Area 14,358 sq km **Population** 3,358,000
Capital Hartford **Largest city** Bridgeport

6 Bucking bronco at a rodeo in the American West

DELAWARE
Area 6447 sq km **Population** 692,000
Capital Dover **Largest city** Wilmington

FLORIDA
Area 170,313 sq km **Population** 13,630,000
Capital Tallahassee **Largest city** Jacksonville

GEORGIA
Area 153,953 sq km **Population** 6,795,000
Capital and largest city Atlanta

HAWAII
Area 28,313 sq km **Population** 1,159,000
Capital and largest city Honolulu

IDAHO
Area 216,456 sq km **Population** 1,026,000
Capital and largest city Boise

ILLINOIS
Area 150,007 sq km **Population** 11,640,000
Capital Springfield **Largest city** Chicago

INDIANA
Area 94,328 sq km **Population** 5,667,000
Capital and largest city Indianapolis

IOWA
Area 145,754 sq km **Population** 2,821,000
Capital and largest city Des Moines

KANSAS
Area 213,110 sq km **Population** 2,539,000
Capital Topeka **Largest city** Wichita

KENTUCKY
Area 104,665 sq km **Population** 3,745,000
Capital Frankfort **Largest city** Louisville

LOUISIANA
Area 134,275 sq km **Population** 4,282,000 **Capital** Baton Rouge **Largest city** New Orleans

MAINE
Area 91,653 sq km **Population** 1,257,000
Capital Augusta **Largest city** Portland

MARYLAND
Area 32,135 sq km **Population** 4,975,000
Capital Annapolis **Largest city** Baltimore

MASSACHUSETTS
Area 27,337 sq km **Population** 6,103,000 **Capital and largest city** Boston

I Hoover Dam

MICHIGAN
Area 250,738 sq km **Population** 9,488,000
Capital Lansing **Largest city** Detroit

MINNESOTA
Area 225,182 sq km **Population** 4,513,000
Capital St. Paul **Largest city** Minneapolis

MISSISSIPPI
Area 125,443 sq km **Population** 2,616,000
Capital and largest city Jackson

NEW HAMPSHIRE
Area 24,219 sq km **Population** 1,154,000
Capital Concord **Largest city** Manchester

NEW JERSEY
Area 22,590 sq km **Population** 7,898,000
Capital Trenton **Largest city** Newark

NEW MEXICO
Area 314,939 sq km **Population** 1,590,000
Capital Santa Fe **Largest city** Albuquerque

NEW YORK
Area 141,089 sq km **Population** 18,350,000
Capital Albany **Largest city** New York

NORTH CAROLINA
Area 139,397 sq km **Population** 6,846,000
Capital Raleigh **Largest city** Charlotte

NORTH DAKOTA
Area 183,123 sq km **Population** 632,000
Capital Bismarck **Largest city** Fargo

OHIO
Area 116,103 sq km **Population** 11,025,000
Capital and largest city Columbus

OKLAHOMA
Area 181,049 sq km **Population** 3,205,000
Capital and largest city Oklahoma City

OREGON
Area 254,819 sq km **Population** 2,949,000
Capital Salem **Largest city** Portland

PENNSYLVANIA
Area 119,291 sq km **Population** 12,105,000
Capital Harrisburg **Largest city** Philadelphia

RHODE ISLAND
Area 4002 sq km **Population** 1,026,000
Capital and largest city Providence

SOUTH CAROLINA
Area 82,898 sq km **Population** 3,616,000
Capital and largest city Columbia

SOUTH DAKOTA
Area 199,745 sq km **Population** 718,000
Capital Pierre **Largest city** Sioux Falls

TENNESSEE
Area 109,158 sq km **Population** 5,026,000
Capital Nashville **Largest city** Memphis

TEXAS
Area 695,676 sq km **Population** 17,610,000
Capital Austin **Largest city** Houston

UTAH
Area 219,902 sq km **Population** 1,795,000
Capital and largest city Salt Lake City

2 Autumn scene in New England

VT. VERMONT
N.H. NEW HAMPSHIRE
CONN. CONNECTICUT
R.I. RHODE ISLAND
N.J. NEW JERSEY
DEL. DELAWARE
MD. MARYLAND

3 Whale-watching off the Atlantic coast

VERMONT
Area 24,903 sq km **Population** 590,000
Capital Montpelier **Largest city** Burlington

VIRGINIA
Area 110,771 sq km **Population** 6,411,000
Capital Richmond **Largest city** Virginia Beach

WASHINGTON
Area 184,674 sq km **Population** 5,052,000
Capital Olympia **Largest city** Seattle

WEST VIRGINIA
Area 62,759 sq km **Population** 1,795,000
Capital and largest city Charleston

WISCONSIN
Area 169,653 sq km **Population** 5,000,000
Capital Madison **Largest city** Milwaukee

WYOMING
Area 253,349 sq km **Population** 462,000
Capital and largest city Cheyenne

★ Capital city
☆ State capital

MISSOURI
Area 180,546 sq km **Pop.** 5,231,000 **Capital** Jefferson City **Largest city** Kansas City

MONTANA
Area 380,850 sq km **Population** 821,000
Capital Helena **Largest city** Billings

NEBRASKA
Area 200,358 sq km **Population** 1,615,000
Capital Lincoln **Largest city** Omaha

NEVADA
Area 286,368 sq km **Population** 1,308,000
Capital Carson City **Largest city** Las Vegas

5 Cliff Palace, built by the Pueblo people

4 The Statue of Liberty in New York harbour

MEXICO
AND CENTRAL AMERICA

MEXICO and the Central American countries link the continents of North and South America. Much of the land is mountainous. There are more than one hundred active volcanoes and many earthquakes occur.

Most Mexicans are *mestizos*, descended from the Native Americans and the Spaniards who conquered Mexico in 1521. The central plateau, where the climate is milder and the land is more fertile than in the dry scrublands to the north, has the

6 Arenal, a volcano in the Costa Rican rainforest

highest population. The capital, Mexico City, is growing rapidly and is now the largest city in the world. In the north, thousands of Mexicans attempt to cross into the United States each day in search of work.

Farther south, the Central American countries are also Spanish-speaking *mestizo* nations, although black West Indians live along the Caribbean coast. Coffee and bananas are the chief crops.

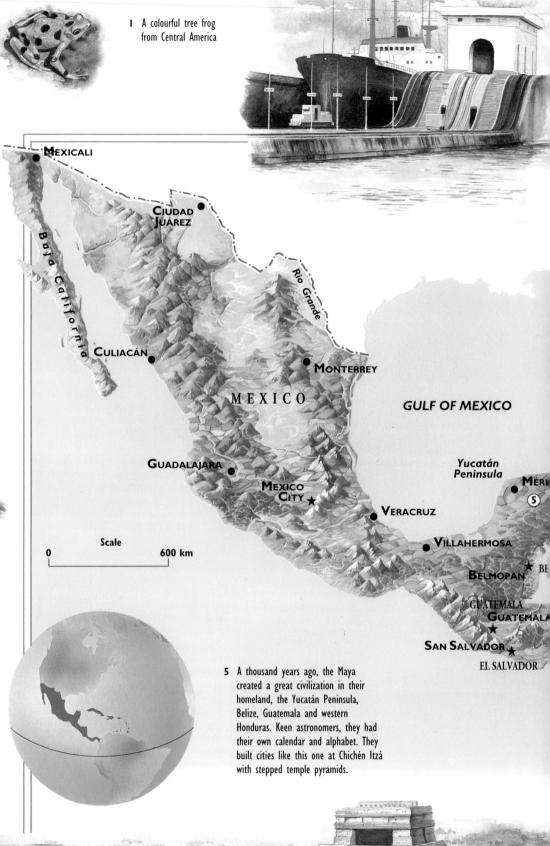

1 A colourful tree frog from Central America

MEXICALI

CIUDAD JUÁREZ

Baja California

Río Grande

CULIACÁN

MONTERREY

M E X I C O

GULF OF MEXICO

GUADALAJARA

Yucatán Peninsula

MÉRI...

(5)

MEXICO CITY ★

VERACRUZ

VILLAHERMOSA

BELMOPAN ★ BE...

GUATEMALA
GUATEMALA ★

SAN SALVADOR ★

EL SALVADOR

Scale

0 — 600 km

5 A thousand years ago, the Maya created a great civilization in their homeland, the Yucatán Peninsula, Belize, Guatemala and western Honduras. Keen astronomers, they had their own calendar and alphabet. They built cities like this one at Chichén Itzá with stepped temple pyramids.

2 Opened in 1914, the Panama Canal cuts through the neck of land, only 65 km wide, that separates the Atlantic and Pacific Oceans. Small locomotives guide the ocean-going ships through the locks.

3 The Caribbean Islands are fringed by coral reefs. Some have become marine parks, complete with underwater nature trails.

CARIBBEAN ISLANDS

MANY ISLAND NATIONS form a ring around the Caribbean Sea. The larger islands of Cuba, Hispaniola, Puerto Rico and Jamaica are known as the Greater Antilles. The remaining smaller islands make up the Lesser Antilles. Lying in the path of easterly winds,

4 Winnowing rice grains in Haiti. The edible grain falls to the ground while the husks remain in the sieve.

the islands enjoy a wet, tropical climate, but sometimes suffer from violent hurricanes.

Very few of the Native Americans survive today. The mixed population is made up of Africans who were brought to the Caribbean to work as slaves on the sugar plantations, Spanish colonizers, and later immigrants from Europe and Asia.

LESSER ANTILLES

A VIRGIN IS. (Br. & US)
B ST. MARTIN (France & Neths)
C ANGUILLA (Br.)
D ST. KITTS AND NEVIS
E ANTIGUA AND BARBUDA
F GUADELOUPE (France)
G DOMINICA
H MARTINIQUE (France)
I ST. LUCIA
J ST. VINCENT AND THE GRENADINES
K BARBADOS
L GRENADA
M TRINIDAD AND TOBAGO
N NETHERLANDS ANTILLES (Neths)

BAHAMAS

HAVANA

CUBA

DOMINICAN REPUBLIC

HAITI ④

JAMAICA

PORT-AU-PRINCE

KINGSTON

SANTO DOMINGO

Hispaniola

SAN JUAN

PUERTO RICO (US)

A
C
B
E
D
F
G
H
③ I
J K
L
M
N

HONDURAS

UCIGALPA

NICARAGUA ①

NAGUA

CARIBBEAN SEA

COSTA RICA

É

⑥

PANAMA

② **PANAMA**

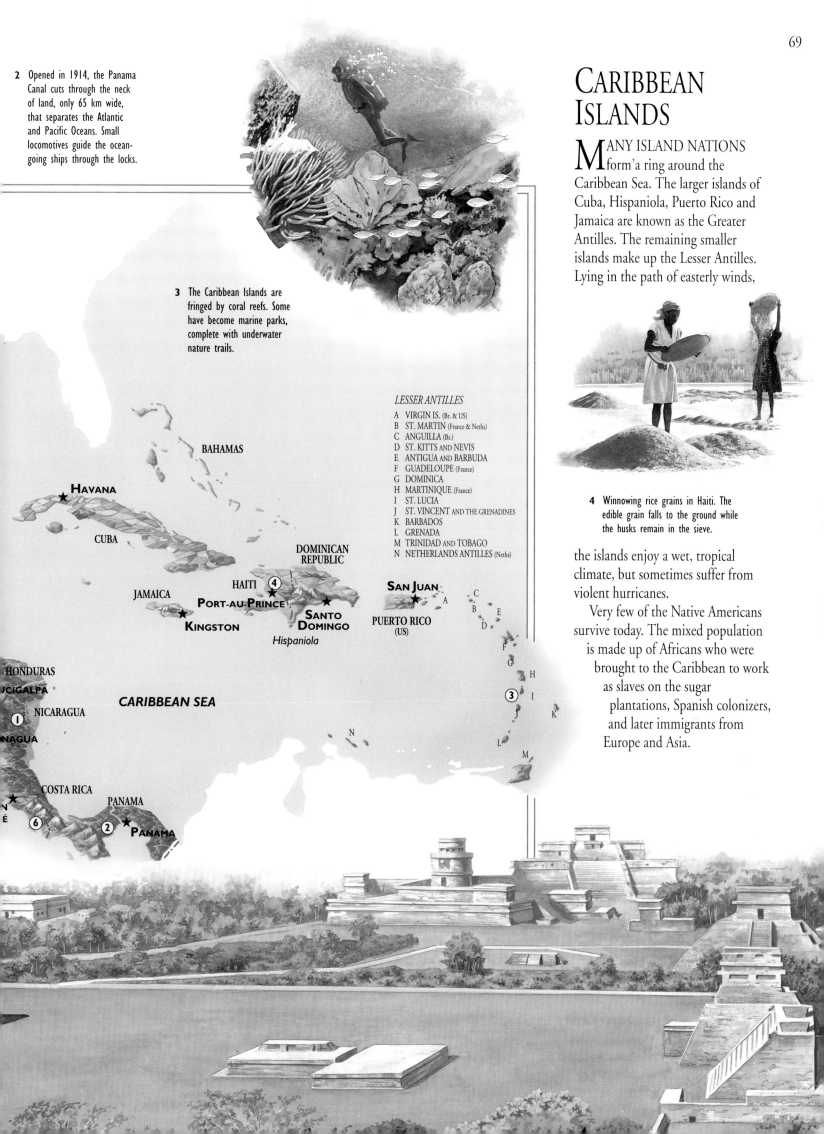

SOUTH AMERICA

SOUTH AMERICA reaches from the tropical coast of the Caribbean to the icy seas of the Antarctic, just 800 km south of Cape Horn. It is joined to North America at the border between Colombia and Panama by a thin neck of land about 150 km wide.

Running the length of the continent are the Andes Mountains, the longest range on Earth. They are home to many Native Americans, descendants of the Incas whose empire once stretched from present-day Colombia to Argentina. To the east lie vast river basins. The largest, occupying more than a third of the continent, is the Amazon basin.

Most of South America's population live in the east of the continent. Apart from Brazil, where Portuguese is spoken, and the Guianas, Spanish is the main language. Much of South America was once under Spanish rule. The people themselves are descended from the Native Americans, Spanish and Portuguese settlers, immigrants from other parts of Europe, and African slaves.

FACTS ABOUT SOUTH AMERICA

Area 17,663,000 sq km
Population 310,700,000
Highest point Aconcagua (Argentina) 6960 m
Lowest point Salinas Chicas (Argentina) 42 m below sea level

Longest river Amazon 6451 km
Largest lake Titicaca (Peru and Bolivia) 8340 sq km
Largest country Brazil 8,511,996 sq km
Largest population Brazil 153,322,000
Largest city São Paulo (Brazil) 10,063,110 people

BRAZIL

ECUADOR

PERU

BOLIVIA

PARAGUAY

URUGUAY

ARGENTINA

CHILE

FRENCH GUIANA

SURINAME

GUYANA

VENEZUELA

COLOMBIA

1 Native American girl from Amazon rainforest, Brazil

3 Native American girl from the Andes, Bolivia

ATLANTIC OCEAN

Equator

Sugar cane

Manatee

Bananas

Cocoa

Vampire bat

Mining

Armadillo

B R A Z I L

Piranha

Capybara

Hummingbird

Amazon

Spider monkey

Anaconda

Mining

SURINAME

FRENCH GUIANA

GUYANA

VENEZUELA

Cattle

Oil

Giant anteater

COLOMBIA

Sloth

Coffee

Jaguar

BOLIVIA

P E R U

Cocoa

ECUADOR

Mining

Potatoes

Fishing

NATIONS OF SOUTH AMERICA

ARGENTINA
Area 2,766,889 sq km **Population** 32,370,000 **Capital** Buenos Aires **Language** Spanish

BOLIVIA
Area 1,098,581 sq km **Population** 7,612,000 **Capitals** La Paz, Sucre **Languages** Spanish, Quechua, Aymara

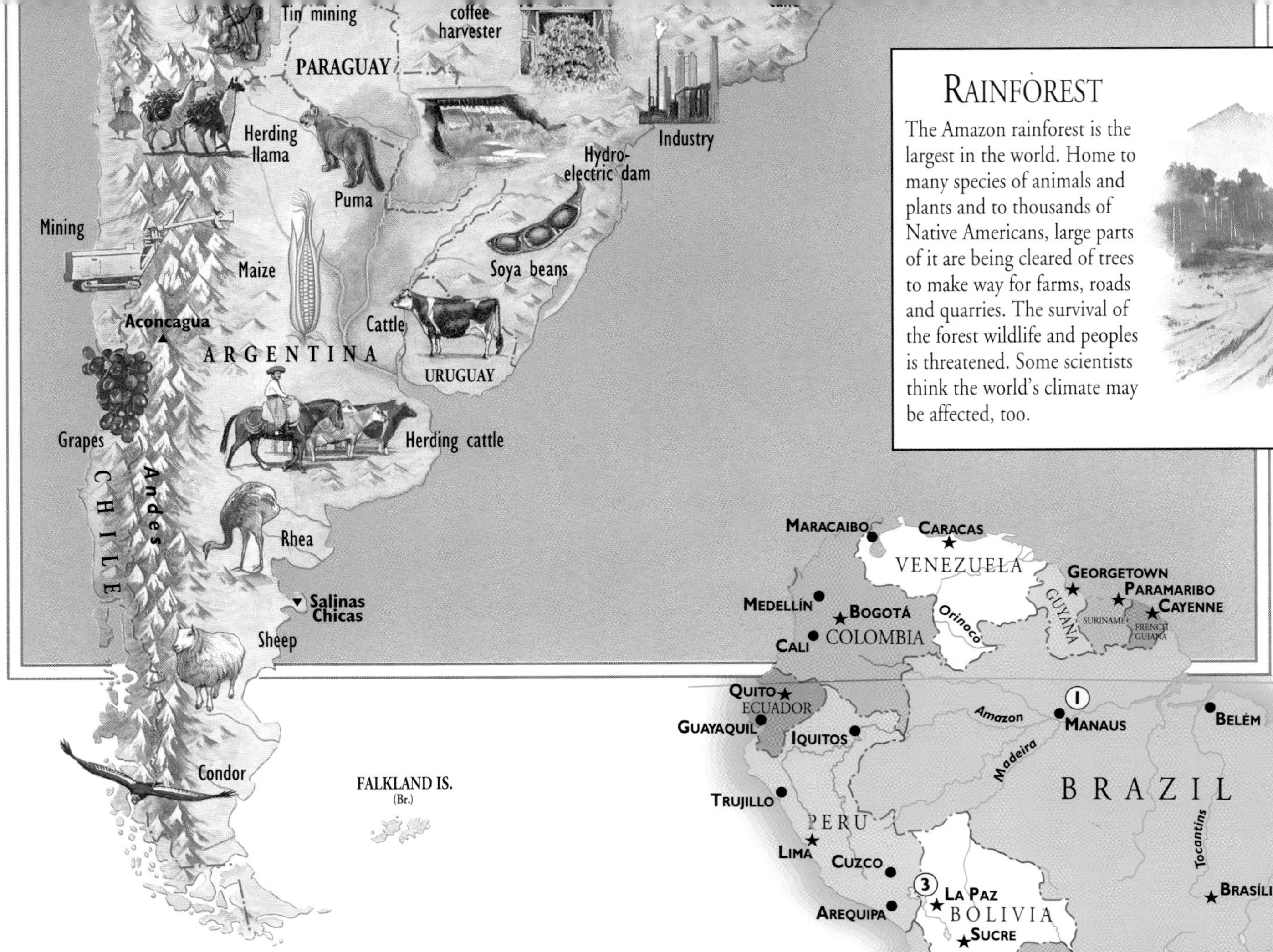
Tin mining
coffee harvester
PARAGUAY
Herding llama
Puma
Hydro-electric dam
Industry
Mining
Maize
Soya beans
Aconcagua
ARGENTINA
Cattle
URUGUAY
Grapes
Herding cattle
CHILE
Andes
Rhea
Salinas Chicas
Sheep
Condor
FALKLAND IS. (Br.)

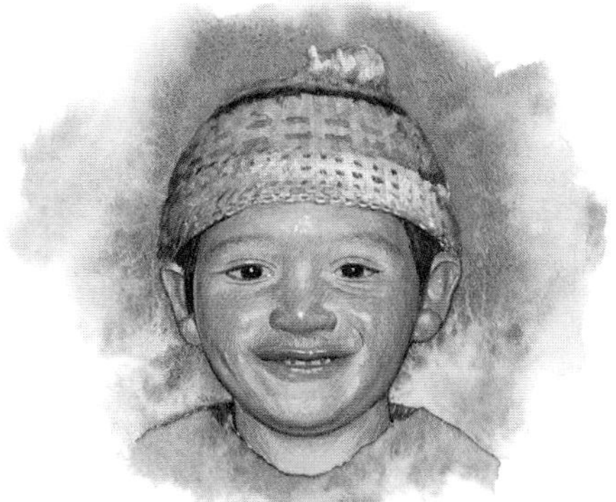

2 Chilean boy

RAINFOREST

The Amazon rainforest is the largest in the world. Home to many species of animals and plants and to thousands of Native Americans, large parts of it are being cleared of trees to make way for farms, roads and quarries. The survival of the forest wildlife and peoples is threatened. Some scientists think the world's climate may be affected, too.

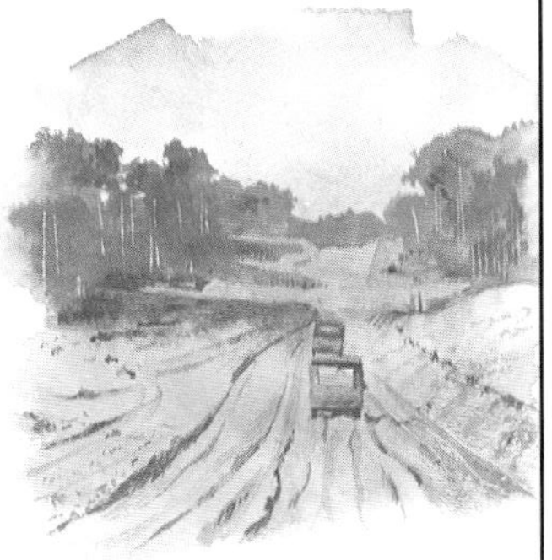

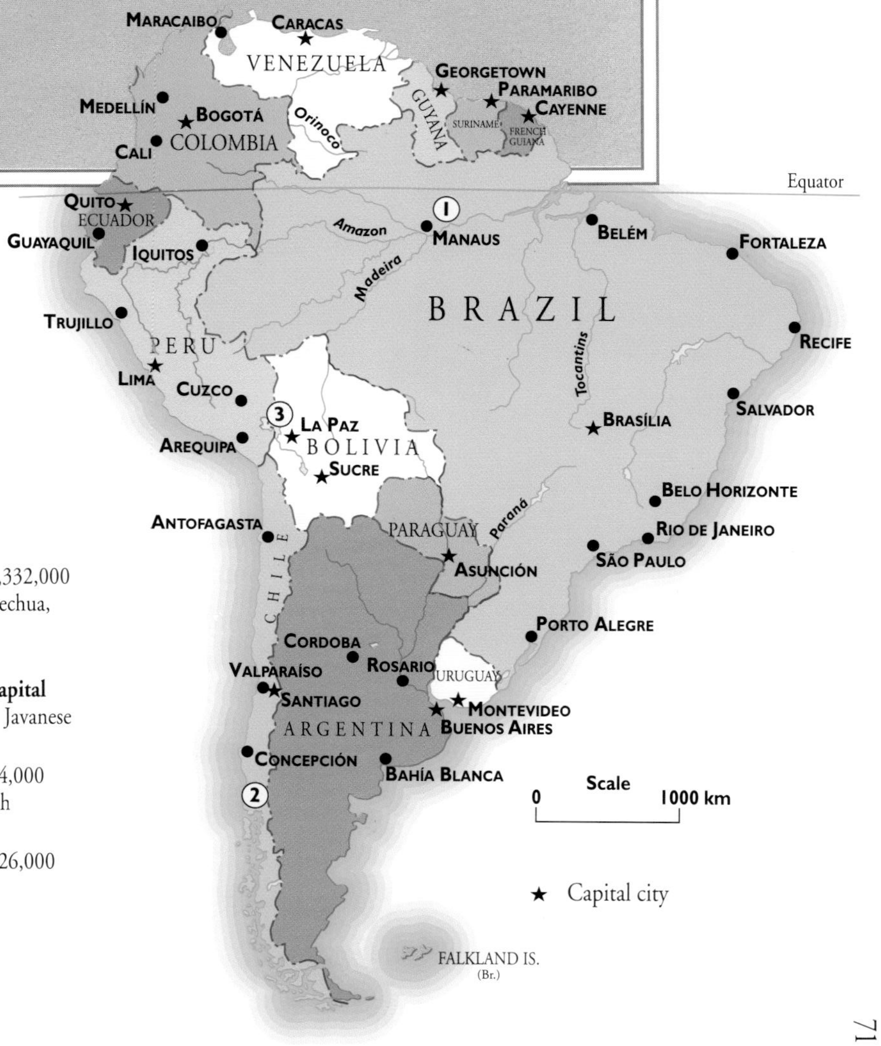
MARACAIBO
CARACAS
VENEZUELA
GEORGETOWN
PARAMARIBO
CAYENNE
MEDELLÍN
BOGOTÁ
Orinoco
GUYANA
SURINAME
FRENCH GUIANA
CALI
COLOMBIA
Equator
QUITO
ECUADOR
Amazon
MANAUS
BELÉM
FORTALEZA
GUAYAQUIL
IQUITOS
Madeira
BRAZIL
TRUJILLO
PERU
Tocantins
RECIFE
LIMA
CUZCO
LA PAZ
BOLIVIA
BRASÍLIA
SALVADOR
AREQUIPA
SUCRE
BELO HORIZONTE
ANTOFAGASTA
PARAGUAY
Paraná
RIO DE JANEIRO
ASUNCIÓN
SÃO PAULO
CHILE
PORTO ALEGRE
CORDOBA
VALPARAÍSO
ROSARIO
URUGUAY
SANTIAGO
MONTEVIDEO
ARGENTINA
BUENOS AIRES
CONCEPCIÓN
BAHÍA BLANCA
Scale
0
1000 km
Capital city
FALKLAND IS. (Br.)

BRAZIL
Area 8,511,996 sq km **Population** 153,322,000 **Capital** Brasília **Language** Portuguese

CHILE
Area 756,626 sq km **Population** 13,599,000 **Capital** Santiago **Language** Spanish

COLOMBIA
Area 1,141,748 sq km **Population** 32,841,000 **Capital** Bogotá **Language** Spanish

ECUADOR
Area 272,045 sq km **Population** 11,078,000 **Capital** Quito **Languages** Spanish, Quechua

FALKLAND ISLANDS
Area 12,173 sq km **Population** 2000 **Capital** Stanley **Language** English

FRENCH GUIANA
Area 91,000 sq km **Pop.** 115,000 **Capital** Cayenne **Languages** French, Creole

GUYANA
Area 214,969 sq km **Population** 740,000 **Capital** Georgetown **Languages** English, Hindi, Urdu

PARAGUAY
Area 406,752 sq km **Population** 4,397,000 **Capital** Asunción **Languages** Spanish, Guarani

PERU
Area 1,285,216 sq km **Population** 22,332,000 **Capital** Lima **Languages** Spanish, Quechua, Aymara

SURINAME
Area 163,265 sq km **Pop.** 400,000 **Capital** Paramaribo **Languages** Dutch, Hindi, Javanese

URUGUAY
Area 176,215 sq km **Population** 3,094,000 **Capital** Montevideo **Language** Spanish

VENEZUELA
Area 912,050 sq km **Population** 20,226,000 **Capital** Caracas **Language** Spanish

COLOMBIA, VENEZUELA AND THE GUIANAS

THE COUNTRIES of northernmost South America all have tropical climates. In the west, the Andes mountains begin their long journey to the southern tip of the continent. Three branches, or *cordilleras*, meet in Colombia. Most of the population live in the cooler climates of the high Andes valleys.

In Venezuela, the Andes reach the coast. Inland, the Orinoco river flows across grassland plains, known as *llanos*, where cattle graze. The Guiana Highlands, a high, flat-topped range, lie across south-east Venezuela and

Guyana. Thick forest grows on their lower slopes, a region little known to the rest of the world.

Mining is important to the countries of this region. Oilfields beneath Lake Maracaibo are important to Venezuela. Colombia has oil, gas and coal, and is the world's largest supplier of emeralds. Plantations of sugar, cotton and bananas were run by Europeans in the Guianas (Guyana, Suriname and French Guiana). Bauxite, the rock from which the metal aluminium is made, is now a valuable export for both Guyana and Suriname.

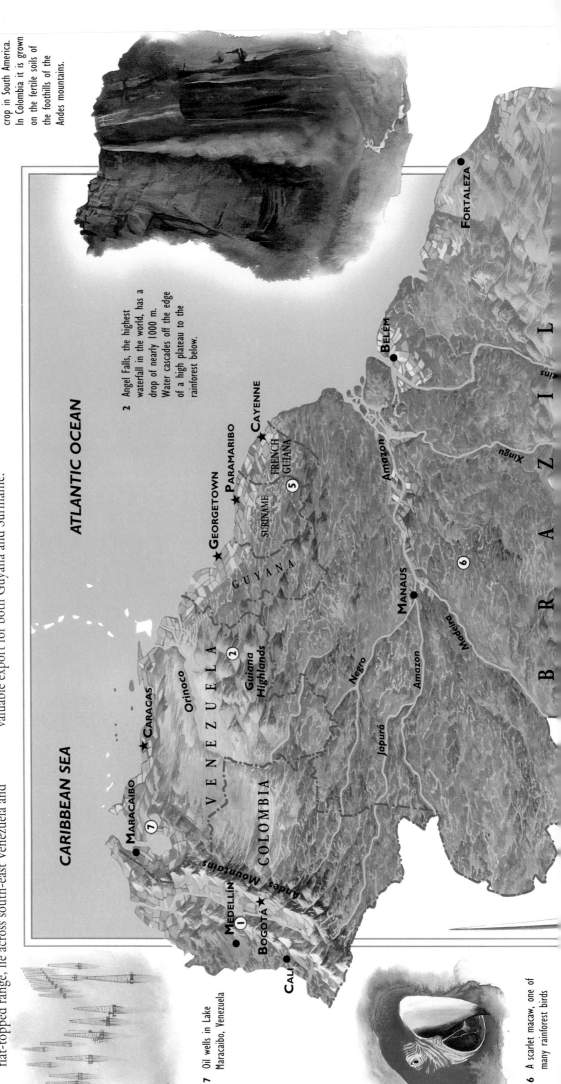

1 Coffee is an important crop in South America. In Colombia it is grown on the fertile soils of the foothills of the Andes mountains.

2 Angel Falls, the highest waterfall in the world, has a drop of nearly 1000 m. Water cascades off the edge of a high plateau to the rainforest below.

7 Oil wells in Lake Maracaibo, Venezuela

6 A scarlet macaw, one of many rainforest birds

CARIBBEAN SEA

ATLANTIC OCEAN

MARACAIBO

CARACAS

Orinoco

VENEZUELA

GUYANA

GEORGETOWN

PARAMARIBO

SURINAME

FRENCH GUIANA

CAYENNE

Guiana Highlands

COLOMBIA

MEDELLIN

BOGOTA

CALI

Andes Mountains

Japurá

Negro

Amazon

MANAUS

Amazon

Madeira

Xingu

BELÉM

FORTALEZA

B R A Z I L

BRAZIL

BRAZIL is South America's largest and most populous nation. It is the fifth largest country in the world. In the north, the world's largest rainforest covers the vast basin of the Amazon river. One fifth of the world's freshwater is carried by the Amazon out to sea. To the south and east of the central highlands lies most of Brazil's farmland. Most Brazilians live in the crowded cities of this region. They are a mixed population, descended from the first Portuguese settlers, black African slaves forced to work on the sugar plantations, and later immigrants from Europe and Asia. Today, coffee, cocoa, soya beans and beef cattle are Brazil's main farm products. Iron mined in the highlands is also an important export.

3 A dancer at the Mardi Gras carnival in Rio de Janeiro

Scale

0   400 km

SALVADOR

BELO HORIZONTE

São Francisco

RIO DE JANEIRO

BRASÍLIA ★

CAMPINAS

SÃO PAULO

CURITIBA

Paraná

PORTO ALEGRE

5 The traditional way of life of many Amazon Native Americans (*left*) looks doomed. Some parts of the forest are being cut down to make way for farmland, quarries and roads. Many native people are leaving the forest to look for work in the towns.

4 Rio de Janeiro (*below*) grew up in the 19th century as a port trading gold and diamonds mined inland. Today it is a rich industrial city with magnificent beaches and views. But all around the city, poor people live in crowded shantytowns.

ECUADOR, PERU AND BOLIVIA

R ISING BETWEEN THE COAST and the Amazon rainforest, the Andes Mountains run through the countries of Ecuador, Peru and Bolivia.

Until it fell to the Spanish invading army in 1532, the Inca Empire once ruled over this land. Today, many Native Americans live high in the mountains, farming on terraced fields cut like steps into the slopes and grazing their animals as they have done for hundreds of years.

In Peru and Ecuador most of the population, descended from both the Native Americans and the Spanish, lives on the coastal plain. There are rich fishing grounds off the coast. Further south the plain turns to desert.

Farther south in Bolivia, between the snow-capped Andean peaks, lies the *altiplano*, a high plain, cold and windswept, where farmers herd llama and alpaca for their meat and wool.

For all three countries, mining is an important source of wealth. Ecuador has oil reserves, Peru produces copper and tin is mined in Bolivia.

PARAGUAY

West of the Paraguay River lies the marshy scrubland of the Gran Chaco. Most of the farmland and population is found in the more fertile east. Many Paraguayans are the descendants of Spanish settlers and Guarani Native Americans.

1 A rope bridge across a deep ravine in the Andes (*above, left*)

2 The Incas built cities, fortresses and temples. Many were destroyed by the conquering Spaniards, but they never found Machu Picchu (*right*). Two thousand metres above sea level, the ruined city was discovered only in 1911.

GALÁPAGOS ISLANDS
(Ecuador)

7 The Galápagos islands are famous for the unique plants and animals that live there. They include marine iguanas, penguins and giant tortoises (*above*).

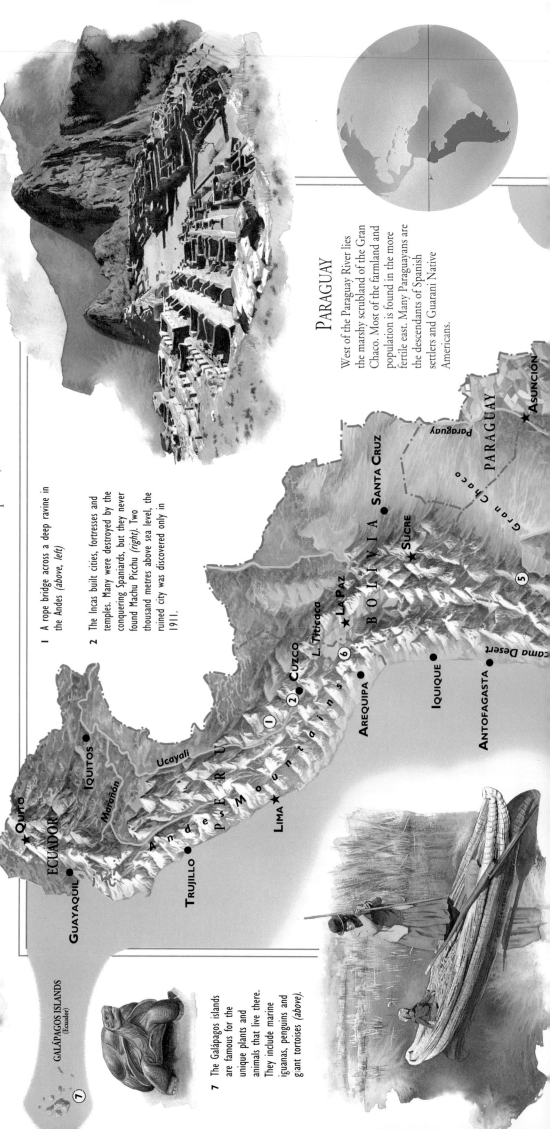

6 A Native American woman rows a reed boat on Lake Titicaca (*above*).

5 The 'Train of the Clouds' crosses the viaduct of Polvorilla in northern Argentina (*below*).

on the Argentinian pampas were herded by gauchos on horseback, the 'cowboys' of South America. Their traditional way of life is disappearing.

PACIFIC
OCEAN

ATLANTIC
OCEAN

4 Guanacos, the wild relatives of llamas and alpacas, still survive in the wild in the remote mountains of southern Chile.

MONTEVIDEO

URUGUAY

★ Río de la Plata

SANTA FE

CORDOBA

ROSARIO

★ BUENOS AIRES

③

MAR DEL PLATA

● BAHÍA BLANCA

P a m p a s

A R G E N T I N A

Aconcagua

MENDOZA

★ SANTIAGO

C H I L E

VALPARAÍSO

CONCEPCIÓN

Andes Mountains

P A T A G O N I A

● COMODORO RIVADAVIA

④

FALKLAND ISLANDS
(Br.)

Magellan's Strait

Tierra del Fuego

Cape Horn

Scale

0   400 km

URUGUAY

Uruguay is a land of low grassy plains grazed by beef cattle. Most of its people are descended from Spanish and Italian settlers. More than half live in the port of Montevideo, its capital.

CHILE AND ARGENTINA

THE ANDES CONTINUE as far as the stormy waters of Cape Horn at the southern tip of South America. The boundary between Chile and Argentina runs along its highest ridge and close to its highest peak, Aconcagua.

Chile is a very long, thin country, 25 times longer than it is wide. Along the northern coastal strip lies the Atacama Desert, the driest region on Earth, where it almost never rains. Here are copper mines, which provide a large part of Chile's exports. Most of the population lives on the warm and fertile central plain.

Immigrants mostly from Italy and Spain arrived in Argentina in the mid-nineteenth century. They settled on the fertile grasslands called the *pampas*, where they farmed wheat and raised cattle. Today, though Argentina has modern industries, beef and grain are still its main produce and most of the population still lives near the *pampas*.

THE POLES

THE NORTHERNMOST and southernmost regions of the world are covered by ice and snow. The Arctic, in the north, is not land at all, but an ocean. Most of it is permanently covered by an ice cap. In winter, the rest is frozen over by rafts of floating ice, called pack ice. Greenland and some islands are also ice-covered throughout the year, while other Arctic lands are low-lying, treeless places. In these tundra regions, where the deeper soils are always frozen, plants and flowers can grow in summer, allowing many different kinds of animals to live there.

Separated from the rest of the world by the Southern Ocean, the continent of Antarctica is about twice

7 An icebreaker is designed to break up the ice as it makes its way across ocean pack ice.

the size of Australia. Inhabited only by people who work at scientific research stations, it is a land of extremes. Nearly the whole landmass is covered by ice and snow all year round. In some parts, the ice is more than 3500 metres deep.

Antarctica is the world's coldest

1 An Arctic animal, the walrus *(left)* may weigh 16 times as much as a human. On land, walruses huddle together in their hundreds.

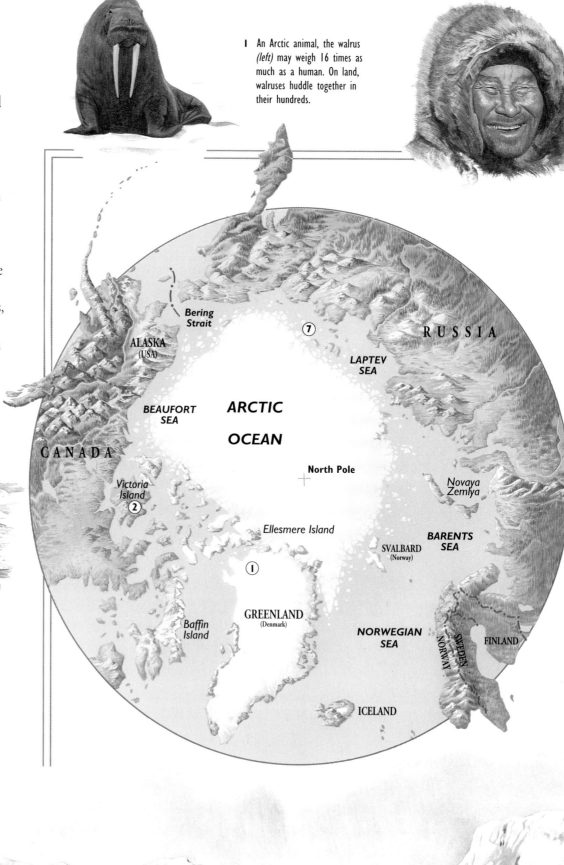

- Bering Strait
- ALASKA (USA)
- BEAUFORT SEA
- CANADA
- Victoria Island ②
- Baffin Island
- GREENLAND (Denmark)
- ① Ellesmere Island
- ⑦
- ARCTIC OCEAN
- North Pole
- RUSSIA
- LAPTEV SEA
- Novaya Zemlya
- SVALBARD (Norway)
- BARENTS SEA
- NORWEGIAN SEA
- NORWAY
- SWEDEN
- FINLAND
- ICELAND

2 The Inuit, or Eskimos *(left)* have lived in the Arctic for thousands of years. For food they have hunted whales, walruses and seals. Their traditional ways of life are changing with the arrival of modern transport and housing.

3 An explorer journeys across the ice with a team of husky dogs *(right)*.

place. It is so cold, boiling water sprayed in the air will turn to ice before it hits the ground! It is hard to imagine that, millions of years ago, Antarctica was covered by hot rainforest, inhabited by hundreds of different kinds of plants and animals. Today, the only animals that live there – whales, penguins, seals and fish – live in the surrounding waters, feeding on krill, tiny shrimp-like creatures that thrive in the cold sea.

④

WEDDELL SEA

QUEEN MAUD LAND

Antarctic Peninsula

⑥

A N T A R C T I C A

③

South Pole
+
⑤

BELLINGSHAUSEN SEA

BYRD LAND

Ross Ice Shelf

WILKES LAND

ROSS SEA

Scale
0   500 km

SOUTHERN OCEAN

4 The humpback whale is famous for its singing. One is seen here flinging itself out of the water, or 'breaching'.

5 This is the South Pole *(below)*. Today, a modern research station is sited there, manned by scientists.

6 Emperor penguins gather together on an Antarctic shore fringed by mountains. Floating out to sea is an iceberg, a block of ice that has broken away from the ice shelf, the frozen waters of an Antarctic bay.

PICTURE INDEX

MAP INDEX

1000 Gair Cyntaf Sali Mali

Haf Llewelyn

Lluniau gan
Simon Bradbury

Gomer

CCBC
PO10293564

Cyhoeddwyd yn 2012 gan Wasg Gomer, Llandysul, Ceredigion SA44 4JL

ISBN 978 1 84851 453 9

Dymuna'r cyhoeddwyr gydnabod cymorth Adrannau Cyngor Llyfrau Cymru.

Argraffwyd a rhwymwyd gan Wasg Gomer, Llandysul, Ceredigion SA44 4JL
www.gomer.co.uk

Cynnwys

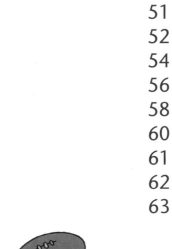

jwg

mop

torth

llwy bren

sosban

tostiwr

tebot

mwg

brwsh llawr

Yn y gegin

cadair

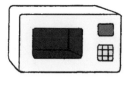
meicrodon

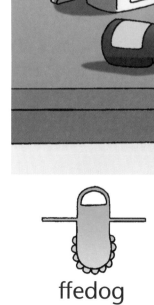
ffedog

padell ffrio

plât

peiriant golchi dillad

bwrdd

silff

bwced mop

powlen

brechdan

sychwr dillad

fforc

cwpwrdd llestri

cwpan

llwy

tegell

rhewgell

sinc

cyllell

cacen

ffwrn/popty

7

cwpwrdd
dillad

 lamp

 cwpwrdd
dillad

 bwrdd
gwisgo

cist
deganau

 gŵn
llofft

Yn y tŷ

gwely

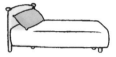

cwilt

tedi

potel dŵr
poeth

lamp

soffa

rheiddiadur

bwrdd bach

silff lyfrau

ffôn

cadair
esmwyth

cadair

argraffydd

lle tân

cawod

bath

clorian

sebon

past
dannedd

llen cawod

drych

lliain

toiled

grisiau

stand
cotiau

cadair
siglo

clustog

blwch
lloeren

teledu

darlun

drws

9

can dyfrio

rhaw

cwch gwenyn

ysgol

coeden afalau

malwoden

nyth

sied

buwch goch gota

Yn yr ardd

lawnt

rhaca/ cribyn

piben ddŵr

Wyt ti'n siŵr mai chwyn yw'r rheina, Dwmplen Malwoden?

mwydyn/ pry genwair

whilber/ berfa

tŷ coeden

tŷ gwydr

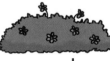
gwely blodau

cennin
Pedr

briallu

lein
ddillad

potiau
blodau

peiriant
torri porfa

rhesi llysiau

pridd

gwenynen

siglen

dant y llew

fforch

colomen

hadau

llithren

gwlithen

lawnt

brwsh

pilipala

casgen ddŵr

11

ffermdy

Ar y fferm

hwrdd/
maharen

byrnau

stabl

mochyn

beic pedair
olwyn

cafn bwyd

ceiliog

dafad

llyn

twlc

ffermwr

tas wair

tarw

bwgan
brain

llo

12

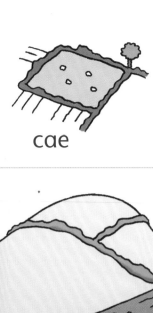
cae

buwch

cwt ieir

cert

gŵydd

ysgubor

sachau

ceffyl

oen bach

wy

cywion

tractor

twrci

ffon fugail

porchell

aradr

cyfrwy

hwyaden

swyddfa post

Yn y dref

stondin marchnad

fan

goleuadau traffig

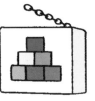
siop deganau

fan bost

Sali Mali a'r Ceffyl Gwyllt

ffordd

siop flodau

archfarchnad

becws

palmant

eglwys

HEDDLU

swyddfa'r heddlu

14

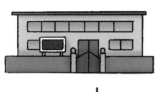
ysgol

stryd

ysbyty

car

llyfrgell

cigydd

capel

sinema

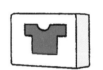
siop ddillad

siop esgidiau

siop trin gwallt

blwch post

car heddlu

Mae angen esgidiau newydd ar Nicw Nacw. I ba siop ddylai fynd?

croesfan

siop lyfrau

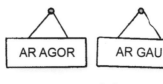
arwyddion

15

Fi fy hun

fy nhafod

fy nhrwyn

fy ngheg

fy ngwefus

fy llygad

fy nghlust

fy nannedd

fy ngwallt

fy ngwddf

fy moch

fy ngên

fy mol

fy nghefn

fy ysgwydd

fy mhen-ôl

fy nghoes

fy mhen-glin

fy ffêr/
fy migwrn

fy
nhroed

fy mraich

fy mys

fy mawd

fy llaw

fy mhenelin

16

Dillad

ffrog

sgert

trowsus

jîns

fest

pants/trôns

sanau

teits

côt

côt law

siaced

hwdi

siwmper

crys

blows

cardigan

crys-T

siorts

het

cap

sgarff

menig

bwcwl

tei

coler

poced

botwm

sip

sandalau

treinyrs

welis

esgidiau

careiau

bwrdd

Yn y dosbarth

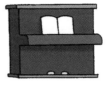
piano

styffylwr

llyfr gwaith

geiriadur

pensil

cyfrifiadur

creonau

clustffonau

taflunydd

sialc

siswrn

brwsh paent

clai

athrawes

twb tywod

tâp selo

tŷ bach twt

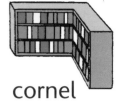

cornel ddarllen

yr wyddor

jig-so

bin ailgylchu

glud

rhifau

siart

pinnau ffelt

cownteri

rhwbiwr

bwrdd gwyn

potiau paent

athro

Y cae chwarae

pêl-droed

pêl rygbi

ffon hoci

potel ddiod

carden goch

gôl-geidwad

pyst rygbi

carden felen

GÔL!
Da iawn ti,
Nicw Nacw.

crys-T

siorts

gôl

chwiban

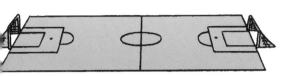

cae pêl-droed

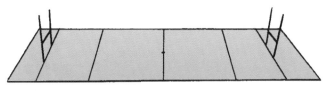

cae rygbi

dyfarnwr

pêl-rwyd

cornel

sanau
pêl-droed

rhwyd

mainc

menig
gôl-geidwad

bag
chwaraeon

esgidiau
pêl-droed

ystafell newid

Fy nheulu i

fi

mam

dad

cath

pysgodyn aur

brawd bach

chwaer

mam-gu/ nain

tad-cu/ taid

ci

modryb

ewyrth

cefnder

cyfnither

hen fam-gu/ hen nain

Priodas

gwas bach

morwyn flodau

morwyn briodas

priodferch

priodfab

gwas priodas

cacen briodas

tusw o flodau

ceffyl a throl

clychau

eglwys

capel

modrwy

conffeti

rhaw

mul/asyn

castell tywod

Ar lan y môr

basged bicnic

sbectol haul

pêl

barcud

gwylan

creigiau

tonnau

cysgodfan

cylch rwber

eli haul

ynys

rhwyf

pwll dŵr

24

seren fôr

ymbarél

cragen

hufen iâ

gwymon

bandiau dŵr

rhwyd

het haul

môr

bwced

cranc

baner

cwch hwylio

goleudy

traeth

cadair haul

bwi

cwch modur

gwely aer

25

cath fôr

llysywen

slefren fôr

tanc ocsigen

cwrel

morlo

dolffin

O dan y dŵr

llongddrylliad

Gwylia'r siarc yna, Nicw Nacw!

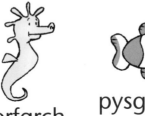

angor

morfarch

pysgodyn

sbwng

masg

siwt rwber

siarc

pysgod

octopws

wystrysen

pysgodyn aur

draenog
y môr

cragen

snorcel

cist drysor

éren fôr

cranc

gwely'r môr

swigod

llong
danfor

morfil

27

Anifeiliaid

gorila

fflamingo

jiráff

arth wen

eliffant

mwnci

parot

broga/llyffant

teigr

cangarŵ

sebra

babŵn

pengwin

tarantiwla

rheino

panda

llygoden

byffalo

camel

arth frown

llew

hipo

lama

bwji

mochyn cwta

crwban

cwningen

ystlum

bochdew

morlo

neidr

estrys

fwltur

eryr

gwdihŵ/tylluan

camelion

crocodeil

Ga' i grocodeil yn anifail anwes, plîs, Sali Mali?

pafiliwn

stondin

Yn yr eisteddfod

llithren

meithrinfa

Mr Urdd

bathodyn

meicroffôn

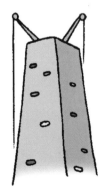

wal ddringo

sticeri

balŵn

ffair

pabell fwyd

lolipop

pabell

ceffylau bach

llwyfan

maes

pabell gelf

fan hufen iâ

pabell ddawns

telyn

olwyn fawr

baner

ceir clatsio

Oes lle am un sticer bach arall?

côr

gwobrau

maes parcio

pabell S4C

beirniad

31

Gwersylla

pabell

caban pren

gwdihŵ/tylluan

carafán

sach gysgu

gwiwer

mynydd

gwialen

rhaeadr

peg

maes carafanau

adlen

ffa pob

balŵn

selsig

cwningen

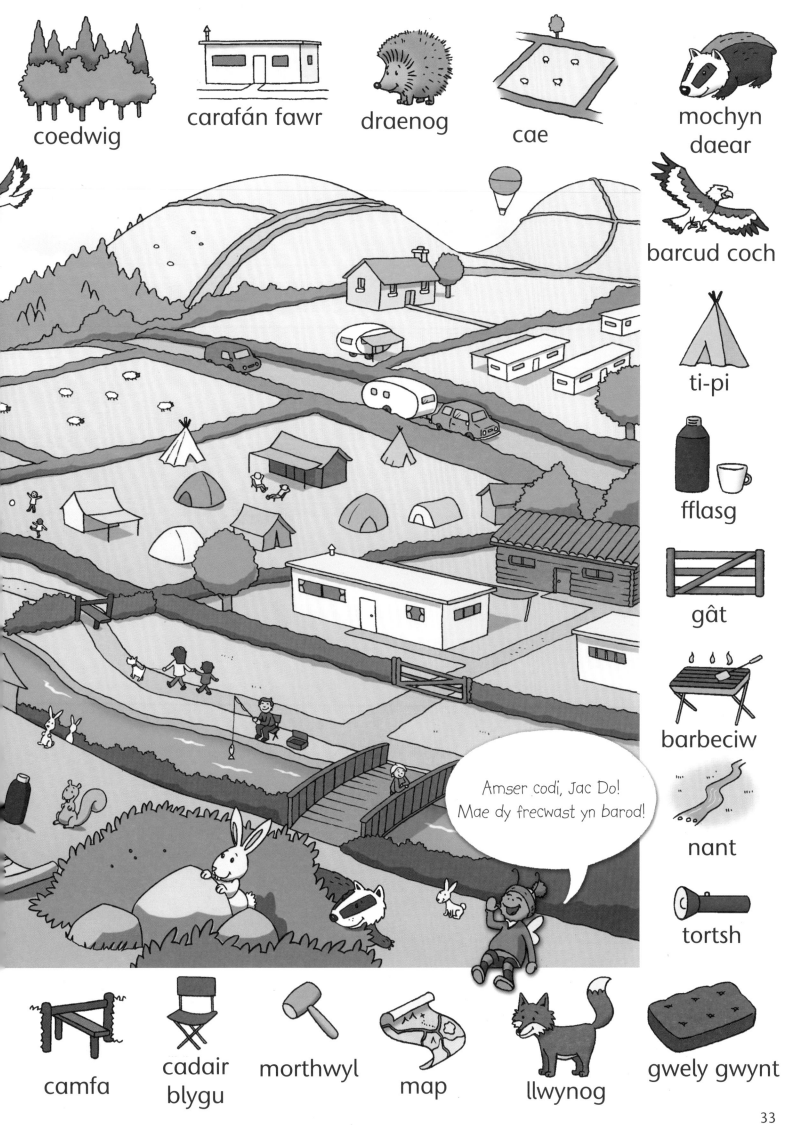

coedwig

carafán fawr

draenog

cae

mochyn daear

barcud coch

ti-pi

fflasg

gât

barbeciw

nant

tortsh

Amser codi, Jac Do!
Mae dy frecwast yn barod!

camfa

cadair blygu

morthwyl

map

llwynog

gwely gwynt

33

O gwmpas Cymru

Glan-llyn

cwch hwylio

canŵ

llyn

siaced achub

cwrs rhaffau

dringwr

helmed

gwregys

wal ddringo

Llangrannog

traeth

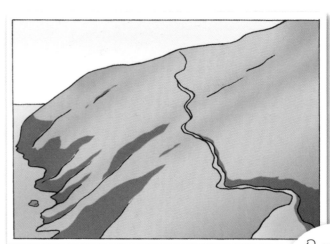

llwybr

O na! Sut mae stopio?

gwibgartio

marchogaeth

sgio

Caerdydd

castell

amgueddfa

pwll nofio

theatr

Canolfan y Mileniwm

crys nos

Teithio

bag molchi

crib

past
dannedd

cês

pasbort

tocyn

bws
deulawr

gorsaf

gyrrwr
trên

sach gefn

bws

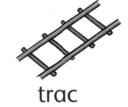
trac

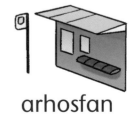
arhosfan

trên

peilot

hofrenydd

awyren

maes awyr

Paid anghofio anfon cerdyn post, Jac y Jwc!

stiwardes

tŵr

tynfad

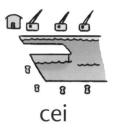

cei

tacsi

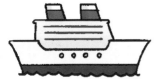

fferi

cwch bach

cwch rhwyfo

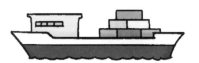

llong nwyddau

parot

cleddyf

trysor

môr-leidr

arian

tywysoges

gorsedd

brenin

castell

Byd ffantasi

coron

llong
môr-ladron

cist
drysor

tywysog

ceffyl
a throl

clogyn

tŵr

brenhines

palas

draig

 het hud

 gwrach

 hudlath

 dewin

hud

 llyfr swynion

 diod hud

 swyn

 crochan

 tylwythen deg

 ysbryd

 ystlum

 hen dŷ

Paid â nychryn i, Sali Mali!

 trên sgrech

 gwe

 pry cop

 hen dŷ

cit adeiladu

Y siop deganau

blociau

beic

doli

tedi

marblis

pyped

jig-sô

dillad doli

gêm fwrdd

sgwter

ceir bach

gêm gyfrifiadur

cardiau snap

jac codi baw

ceffyl siglo

pram

tŷ dol

crud

llestri bach

cadw-mi-gei

barcud

pêl droed

raced

bat a phêl

paent

clai

awyren

car rasio

creonau

roced

41

Swyddi

Beth hoffet ti fod pan fyddi di'n fawr?

adeiladwr

clown

dawnswraig

ffermwr

plymar

saer

meddyg

athrawes

nyrs

plismon

bocsiwr

actor

gweinidog

llyfrgellydd

gofodwr

consuriwr

diffoddwr tân

gyrrwr bws

cogydd

gyrrwr trên

chwaraewr
rygbi

deintydd

postmon

mecanic

ditectif

arlunydd

cerddor

chwaraewr
pêl-droed

fan

Yn y garej

car

beic modur

lorri

pwmp petrol

llyw

cist

cadach

goleuadau

sedd ôl

bonet

sedd flaen

teiars

olwyn

mecanic

helmed

oferôl

golchwr ceir

Siop trin gwallt

 siswrn

 barbwr

 steilydd

 sychwr

 brwsh

 crib

 sythwr

 siampŵ

 drych

 lliain

 cynffon

 Mohican

 gwallt golau

 gwallt tywyll

 gwallt hir

 gwallt cyrliog

 gwallt byr

 gwallt syth

45

Dwi'n gallu . . .

llamu

cerdded

neidio

sglefrio

cropian

llithro

siglo

sgipio

rhedeg

nofio

darllen

arnofio

plymio

dringo

palu

hau

cuddio

dyfrio

chwynnu

cario

dawnsio

canu

yfed

rapio

arllwys/tywallt

peintio

chwilio

adeiladu

cysgu

glanhau

Tywydd

bwrw glaw/glawio

tywallt/arllwys y glaw

glaw mân

gwynt

corwynt

rhew/iâ

bwrw eira

storm

mellt a tharanau

heulog

haul tanbaid

cysgod

cymylog

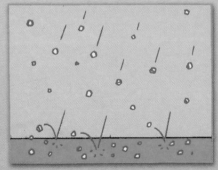

bwrw cenllysg/cesair

niwlog

Lliwiau

Odli

Mae cranc **pinc** yn y **sinc**.

Ga' i frechdan **ham**, plis Mam?

Rhys, rhaid bwyta dy **bys**.

Tyrd o'r **sach**, gwningen **fach**.

Pwy sy fan **acw**, Nicw **Nacw**?

Gwylia'r **rhew**, Pry Bach **Tew**.

Dwmplen Malwoden yn bwyta **letysen**.

Tyrd am **dro**, Jac **Do**.

Rhifau a siapiau

un   haul

dau   sioncyn y gwair

tri   broga/llyffant

pedwar   lindysyn

pump   morgrugyn

chwech   mwydyn/pry genwair

saith   chwilen

wyth   gwlithen

naw   buwch goch gota

deg   hwyaden

un deg un   deilen

un deg dau   brigyn

un deg tri   cwmwl

un deg pedwar   dant y llew

un deg pump   coeden

un deg chwech   carreg

un deg saith   cragen

un deg wyth   pluen

un deg naw   mesen

dau ddeg   weli

cylch   sgwâr   triongl   petryal   pyramid   côn   ciwb

Geiriau croes

golau

tywyll

i fyny

i lawr

blêr

taclus

cas

caredig

bas

dwfn

tal

byr

dof

gwyllt

agor

cau

llyfn

garw

gwag

llawn

chwith dde

meddal

caled

hawdd

anodd

agos

pell

poeth

oer

gwlyb

sych

brwnt/budr

glân

uchel

bach

mawr

isel

hen

newydd

dydd

nos

tew

tenau

Ble wyt ti, Sali Mali?

Dinbych-y-pysgod

Ynys Enlli

Sain Ffagan

Stadiwm y Mileniwm

Froncysylltau

Aberystwyth

Llanberis

Oakwood

Yr Wyddfa

Llanelwedd

Tyddewi

Dan yr Ogof

Pwll Mawr

Ynys Lawd

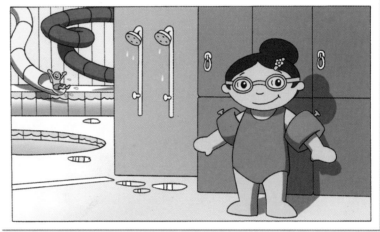

Y Rhyl

Abertawe

Caernarfon

Sycharth

Arberth

Yn yr eira

dyn eira

sled

het wlân

iglw

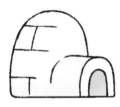
esgidiau
sglefrio

rhaff

llwybr

pluen eira

rhew/iâ

eirfwrdd

angel eira

56

rhaw

titw

traciau

sanau gwlân

lluwch

briwsion

peli eira

robin goch

côt

caseg eira

sgis

bwrdd adar

Rhaid gwisgo'n gynnes
i chwarae yn yr eira.

welis

bryn

pibonwy

sgarff

Y tymhorau

Gaeaf

CHWEFROR

IONAWR

RHAGFYR

Daw Siôn Corn cyn bo hir!

TACHWEDD

HYDREF

Hydref

Oes digon o afalau yn dy fasged?

MEDI

58

Dyddiau'r wythnos

Dyddiadur

Pen blwydd

parti

ffrindiau

balwnau

carden

Pen blwydd Hapus! 5

castell bownsio

pwll peli

pwll padlo

gêmau

rhuban

tâp selo

papur lapio

siswrn

anrheg

canhwyllau

bananas

jeli

ysgytlaeth

cacen

brechdanau

pop

platiau

creision

afalau

grawnwin

mefus

selsig

caws

orenau

Nadolig

lleuad

seren

addurn

sled

Siôn Corn

carw

coeden Nadolig

coron

brenin

stabl

bugail

Y Baban Iesu

preseb

asyn

oen

angel

aur   thus   myrr   Joseff   Mair

Cinio Nadolig

het bapur

twrci

pys

grefi   tatws   moron   pwdin Nadolig   cracer